ESL Classroom Activities for Teens and Adults

SHELLEY ANN VERNON

Please note that this book is written using British English
spelling (with -ize/-yze endings) and punctuation.

# CONTENTS

PART 3

# QUICK START GUIDE AND DETAILED INDEX

**Key**

| | |
|---|---|
| B | beginner |
| I | intermediate |
| A | advanced |
| any language | teach any vocabulary or grammar with this game |
| general language | English in general (not anything specific) |

| | |
|---|---|
| Step 1 | Listening Drills |
| Step 2 | Speaking Drills |
| Step 3 | Spelling, Writing Drills and Reading |
| Step 4 | Listening Games and Activities for Fluency |
| Step 5 | Speaking Games and Activities for Fluency |
| Step 6 | Creative Writing Activities |

## Step 1  Listening Drills

Select from these to introduce vocabulary and grammar.

| Game | Level | Focus |
|---|---|---|
| Alphabet | B | alphabet |
| Bingo | I | any language |
| Dictation | B, I | any language |
| Grammar Knock Out | B, I, A | any language |
| Hand Sign Stories | B, I | any language |
| Higher Or Lower | B | comparatives |
| Simon Says | B, I | vocabulary and commands |
| Treasure Hunt | B, I, A | prepositions, nouns |
| True Or False | B | vocabulary |
| Word Order | B, I | any language |

## Step 2  Speaking Drills

Select from these to drill new grammar or revise it.

| Game | Level | Focus |
|---|---|---|
| A Day In The Life | B | any language |
| Alphabet B | B | alphabet |
| Alphabet War | B, I | alphabet, sentences |
| Battleships | B, I | any language |
| Blow Your House Down | B, I | any language |
| Brainstorm And Rhyming Brainstorm | B, I, A | any language |
| Board Games | B | any language |

| | | |
|---|---|---|
| Comparatives Get In Order | B | comparatives |
| Connect Four | B, I | any language |
| Counting | B | numbers |
| Cryptic Clues | B, I | any language |
| Detective Game | B, I | questions |
| Directions Games | B | basic directions |
| English Trivia | B, I | any language |
| Fill In Drill | B, I, A | any language |
| Find The Pairs | B, I | any language |
| Fizz Buzz | B, I | vocabulary review |
| Good Evening Beach Ball | B, I | easy speaking warm-up |
| Grammar Drill | B, I | any language |
| Guess The Action | B | present and/or past continuous |
| Guess The Price | B, I | currencies and money |
| Guess The Question | B, I | any language |
| I Took A Trip | B | vocabulary and past tense drill |
| Higher Or Lower | B | comparatives |
| Jeopardy | B, I, A | any language |
| Joker | B, I | any language |
| Last Card | B, I | any language |
| Lego Negotiations | B, I | shapes and colours |
| Make A Sentence/Question | B, I, A | any language |
| Match Up | B, I | any language |
| Memory Challenge | B, I | questions |
| Minesweeper | B, I | any language |
| No 'Yes' Or 'No' | B, I | questions and short-form answers |
| Noughts And Crosses | B, I | any language |
| Old Maid | B, I | any language |
| Pairs | B, I | any language |
| Parts Of Speech Path Finder | B, I | any language |
| Personalization | B, I | any language |
| Picture Flashcards | B, I | any language |
| Present Perfect | B, I | present perfect |
| Pyramid | B | any language |
| Relay Race And Variant | B, I, A | any language |
| Rivet | B, I | vocabulary review |
| Rhyming Challenge | I, A | any language |
| Shopping List Memory Game | B, I | any language |
| Solve It | B, I | speaking drill |
| Speed Drill | B, I | any language drill |
| Subject–Verb–Object | B, I | any language |

| | | |
|---|---|---|
| Things We Do | B, I | any language |
| Time Bomb | B, I | any language |
| True Or False Questions | B, I | any question forms |
| Typhoon | B, I | any language |
| Vocabulary Baseball | B, I | any language |
| Vocabulary Repetition | B | vocabulary |
| Which One Has Gone? | B | vocabulary |
| Word Association | I | vocabulary |
| Word Chain – Round The Alphabet | B, I | vocabulary, lower levels |
| Word Chains | I, A | vocabulary, higher levels |
| Zip Zap Vocabulary Revision | B, I | vocabulary |

## Step 3  Spelling, Writing Drills And Reading

Select from these for spelling, grammar writing or reading.

| Game | Level | Focus |
|---|---|---|
| Anagrams | B, I, A | spelling |
| Boggle | B, I, A | spelling and vocabulary |
| Buddy Reading | B, I, A | pair work |
| Build A Sentence | B, I, A | reading and writing |
| Find The Pairs Pronunciation And Spelling | B, I, A | pronunciation and spelling |
| Gap Fill Game | B, I | writing drill |
| Grammar Auction | B, I, A | grammar check |
| Guess The Word | B, I | spelling and vocabulary |
| Peer Editing | B, I, A | any language |
| Poetry | A | – |
| Population Punctuation | B, I, A | reading and sentence construction |
| Punctuation | I, A | Reading |
| Quiz Race | B, I, A | reading |
| Readers' Theatre | B, I | reading |
| Reading Treasure Hunt | B, I | scanning, grammar, vocabulary |
| Remember And Write | B, I | spelling and vocabulary revision |
| Re-Order It | B, I | reading |
| Sequences | B, I, A | spelling |
| Spell And Speak | B, I, A | spelling |
| Spelling Challenge | B, I, A | spelling |
| Stop | B, I | writing, vocabulary |

| | | |
|---|---|---|
| Ten Important Sentences With Watermelon | B, I | any language |
| Tests And Exams | B, I | – |
| Treasure Hunt | B, I | writing clues |
| Vocabulary Picture Hunt | B, I | spelling |
| Vocabulary Scavenger Hunt | B, I | skimming/reading for vocabulary |
| Write It Up | B, I | writing drill |
| Writing Relay | B, I | writing drill |

## Step 4  Listening Fluency

Select from these for listening comprehension.

| Game | Level | Focus |
|---|---|---|
| Guess Who Listening | I | general language |
| Jigsaw Listening | B, I | any language |
| Lyrics And Songs | B, I | – |
| Mad Libs | B, I, A | review of parts of speech/listening |
| Movie Excerpts And Previews | I, A | general language |
| Radio Broadcasts And Transcriptions | I, A | general language |
| Vocabulary Scavenger Hunt Listening | B, I | any language |

## Step 5  Speaking Fluency

Select from these for conversation and fluency.

| Game | Level | Focus |
|---|---|---|
| A Day In The Life | I, A | general language or any specific language |
| Alibi | B, I, A | general language |
| Battleships | I, A | any language |
| Call My Bluff | B, I, A | general language |
| Chants | B, I, A | any language |
| Charades | I | general language |
| Creative Storytelling | I, A | general language |
| Debates | I, A | general language |
| Decision Time | I | conditionals and general language |
| Describe The Picture | B, I | prepositions, there is, there are |
| Describe The Word | I, A | general language |

| | | |
|---|---|---|
| Either Or | I, A | general language |
| Get Moving Creative Vocabulary Game | B, I, A | general language |
| Getting To Know You | B, I, A | talking about people, likes and dislikes |
| Guess The Meaning Of Dates And Numbers | I, A | general language |
| Hot Seat | I, A | Any language |
| How It's Made | B, I, A | general language |
| Interviews | I, A | general language, may be highly structured for lower levels or freer |
| Jeopardy | B, I, A | any language |
| Jokes | I, A | general language |
| Lego Negotiations | B, I, A | negotiating |
| Making Up Stories | B, I, A | general language |
| Match Up | I, A | vocabulary, general language |
| Memory Challenge | B, I | any language |
| Movie Excerpts And Previews | I, A | general language |
| Mystery Bag | I, A | describing things, general language |
| Name The Thing | I, A | asking questions and general language |
| Odd One Out | B,I,A | general language |
| Parts Of Speech Path Finder | B, I, A | any language |
| Persuasion | I, A | general language |
| Picture Inspiration | B, I | any language |
| Presentations | I, A | general language |
| Problem Solving | I, A | general language |
| Pyramid | I, A | any language |
| Qualities | I, A | general language |
| Questionnaires | B, I | any language |
| Quiz | B, I, A | any language |
| Radio Broadcasts And Transcriptions | I, A | general language |
| Role-Plays | B, I, A | general language |
| Round Robin | B, I, A | general language |
| Sentence Play Off | I, A | general language |
| Spontaneous Sentence | I, A | general language |
| Story Dominoes | I, A | general language |
| Story Memory Game | B, I | any language |
| Storytelling | B, I, A | general language |

| Talk About It | I, A | general language |
| Tongue Twisters | B, I, A | general language |
| Triangles Talking Point | I, A | general language |
| Vocabulary Baseball | I, A | vocabulary revision |
| What Or Who Am I? | I, A | general language |
| Why? | I | general language |

## Step 6  Creative Writing

Select from these for writing fluency.

| Game | Level | Focus |
| --- | --- | --- |
| Call My Bluff Definitions | B, I, A | general language |
| Creative Writing | B, I, A | general language |
| Creative Writing Diary Project | B, I, A | general language |
| Creative Writing With Adjectives | B, I, A | general language |
| Movie Game 10 | A | general language |
| Figure It Out | B, I, A | general language |
| Homework | B, I, A | responsible learning |
| Lyrics And Songs | B, I | general language |
| Poetry | A | general language |
| Quiz | B, I, A | any language |
| Quiz Race | B, I, A | any language |
| Sentence Play Off | I, A | general language |
| Summaries | I, A | general language |
| Things | I, A | vocabulary revision/drilling short sentences |

# PART 1

1
## INTRODUCTION

Games in the language classroom are more than just a fun break from worksheets and textbooks. They are important tools for addressing a variety of problems that can impede your students' progress in learning a language. Games help students relax so that gender, cultural barriers and tensions can be broken down. They provide structured independence for beginners, helping them move through the 'silent period', and add flexibility to planning for classes where attendance is unpredictable. They also facilitate learning in different styles, which maximizes your students' chances for absorbing the language. Games allow you, as the teacher, to have students work together while you maintain control over the lesson's content. In short, a good supply of games will make you a more effective teacher than the teacher who sticks slavishly to textbooks, worksheets and artificial pair work interactions.

## Should Teachers Use Games With Teens And Adults?

Walking into a classroom full of adult English language learners can be far more intimidating than facing a class of children. You are there to teach a serious subject, one that may affect your students' careers, hopes for the future and even their ability to survive in a new country. You may not feel that asking students your own age, and sometimes older, to play games is going to help your teaching or their learning, but you couldn't be more wrong. Games can help you overcome numerous roadblocks that stand between your students and their mastery of English.

The main roadblock you may face, as a teacher who might want to use games in the classroom, is your own hesitance about using this approach with adults. However, basically, there is no difference between young and adult learners – we all like to have fun. Classes for adults that contain games are refreshing and allow ample opportunity to communicate and work on speaking fluency.

According to research, many adults feel anxious when learning a foreign or second language. Games can help them forget that they are learning and instead enjoy the experience while enhancing their knowledge. The positive emotions that they experience make them relax and feel more confident. In short, adults can learn through games in language teaching just as much as children. In the words of a Chinese proverb: 'I hear, I forget. I see, I understand and I do, I remember.'

## The Gender Question

All people learn differently, and there are many reasons as to why there is so much variation. Gender is an important factor to consider. There is a tendency for women to be more flexible and for men to be more competitive. The idea that women are more verbal and men more analytical is widely accepted; women are often seen as more contemplative, and men as more active.

Games provide a safe, fun outlet for competitive urges and help keep students from becoming too exam focused. Role-play games, re-enactments and 'murder mysteries', where students have to improvise and play parts outside their everyday lives, create changeable situations that encourage flexible thinking in all students. Those who struggle with test anxiety often attain new levels of fluency in these games because the goal is not to get a good score but to find out 'who did it' or to achieve some goal, such as bargaining with other groups for items they need to fulfil a game's objective.

As most language games combine verbal and analytical elements, male and female students can excel at them. Word puzzles such as Hangman and Rivet, as well as quiz games like Jeopardy, mix language skills with strategic thinking in a way that is fun for everyone. It is not unusual for too-cool-for-school teenage boys to remain silent all through class, but when the games come out suddenly it's all about winning, and they don't mind speaking in English. The girls want to show off as well, and pretty soon you can't keep them quiet!

## The Culture Question

Before including games in a lesson plan, it is important to consider the cultural background of the students you are working with and the cultural setting of your class. Students in multi-cultural classes in an English-speaking country are usually more flexible in their expectations. Start with 'get to know you' games and those that allow your students to examine their preconceptions in a new setting. Riddles inherently require players to look at ordinary things from a different point of view, so riddle contests where students try to stump each other can be fun at the intermediate level. It makes for an interesting cultural lesson if students translate riddles from their own countries. Students solving riddles in teams also makes for a good icebreaker.

Students in mono-cultural classes in their home country will bring their own cultural expectations into class. If you are new to a country, get to know just what these expectations are in regards to adults playing games by asking teachers who have been there for a while and reading up on the local culture before you arrive. Even if you do all this, be sure to get a run-down on individual students from your school administrators or secretaries whenever possible. Adult Japanese students will enjoy all kinds of games from the beginning, partly because party games are a big part of their normal after-work socializing. If you are teaching in Germany, on the other hand, you may run into resistance at first – adult game playing tends to be less rambunctious and language study is considered a very serious endeavour.

Initially, you may need to focus on role-plays in order to get your students ready to step outside of their comfort zones. Treat your classroom as an English culture zone so that students will begin to expect interactions that differ from their own cultures. In this way, games will be less of a surprise. Decorating the walls suitably is always a good way to start, but may not be possible. Bringing in English news magazines and sharing snacks from home are other good ways to set up your culture zone. Comics from English-language papers can lead to some interesting cultural discussions, since many kinds of humour tend to be dependent on cultural norms and expectations.

**Tensions In The Classroom**

Sometimes you will be faced with outside tensions coming into your classroom, so including games in your lessons can help you create safe and interesting interactions among your students. Points of tension within a class can stem from there being a mix of cultural backgrounds, current events such as war and immigration, and students with personal difficulties, including learning disabilities. If you have ever had students from Iraq and Brazil in the same class, it's probably easy to imagine the kinds of tension that can arise between male and female students from different countries. In Britain during the conflict in Bosnia it was not unusual to have many students from each side sharing the same ESL class while recovering from terrible losses, while on the west coast of the United States one still sometimes encounters bitter feelings about World War II held by Chinese or Korean students towards students from Japan.

In these cases, a teacher must constantly balance the need for open-ended communication with creating a comfortable and safe space for learning. Games' highly structured interactions are a vital tool in maintaining this balance and breaking tension. However, in very touchy situations, such as those that can arise with war victims or refugees, avoid 'getting to know you'-type games that use personal information, as these can result in floods of tears. Use made-up scenarios instead. It is also best to hold off on role-plays that are very open ended until you feel you know the students well enough to have a good idea of the direction the exercise will take. It is always better to start with more structure and control and then loosen up as you get a better feel for the class.

Scripted games that feature or drill a particular grammar point (such as the verb review game Things We Do, where the teacher gives a category and students come up with sentences using all the associated verbs they can think of) is a good way to start students practising and working together in a very neutral way. Board games like English Trivia, based on Trivial Pursuit, are good for reviewing both language points and cultural information in a fairly neutral format. Crossword puzzles, Find the Pairs memory game (also known as Pelmanism) and Build-a-Sentence can be played with only very structured student interaction, while goal-oriented role-plays like shopping games where students try to buy a particular set of ingredients can become more open ended and allow the teacher to introduce greater freedom for students while still setting boundaries for the interactions.

## Beginners And Shy Or Anxious Learners

One of the most frustrating things for adult learners is 'the silent period', which usually covers the first three to six months of language learning, during which time students are absorbing a new phonetic system, vocabulary, grammar structure and cultural cues. It's completely normal not to speak much at all during this period: after all, infants spend well over a year not expected to say a thing beyond nonsense babbles. Infants, though, are developing in so many ways that we don't think about their lack of speech, but for adults, who have been successfully communicating for many years in their native tongue, feeling like a toddler linguistically can be extremely frustrating.

Enter the ESL teacher with a great selection of games that not only address the basic skills that all learners need to master, but provide students with the chance to communicate successfully in a highly structured or patterned way with the meaning clearly demonstrated (repetition without comprehension would not be nearly so effective) and integrated into the lesson.

A word on handling learners' shyness and reluctance to speak. You will likely teach students who are shy in life and excruciatingly shy when it comes to speaking English. Putting someone on the spot and trying to force him or her to answer in front of the class – 'Speak up, I can barely hear you! – will get you nowhere. The student may not even show up to your next class. At times, your whole class may be shy about speaking. It can be catching!

In these situations, a good ploy is to use speaking games where everyone is talking together, thus no individuals stand out. There are plenty such activities in this book. Have the whole class chant a poem, a tongue twister or chorus from a song together. Say the given words quietly, loudly, angrily, in a high pitch, a low growl, or whisper them. In this way, no one is exposed, yet everyone has a chance to speak out and be expressive. This can help conquer nerves when it comes to talking in public.

In pairs, have students drill a given short dialogue over and over, using different expressive voices. This repetition builds confidence, fluency and helps conquer shyness.

Games like Round Robin Advice suit the 'silent period' very well, since the students can write out and rehearse their parts of the interactions in advance and only have to select the correct response from the pre-written choices. Other games, like Grammar Auction, put the focus on a non-linguistic goal – making 'money' (points) through bidding on grammatically correct sentences – and will encourage even quiet students to call for your attention because they aren't worried about what they are saying: they are focused on winning the auction.

Games with highly patterned interactions are wonderful for beginners. The game Good Evening Beach Ball not only wakes up your tired businessmen and women, but it takes the pressure off them because when they catch the ball all they have to do is read the phrases to which their thumbs are pointing and then throw the ball to the next person. As I say later, you'll understand what an impact this class opener can have when students begin to wish you 'Good evening!' spontaneously, with no beach ball in sight.

## Unpredictable Class Attendance

Unpredictable attendance in adult ESL classes is common; business classes can be erratic because work schedules can change suddenly. It isn't unusual to have a single student at the start of an evening class (or, on the other hand, to have a full complement of 12 (or 18, or 20 ...). It is a good idea always to have on hand activities that expand and contract easily for those times when you just don't know how many students to expect. Without some preparation, you could run out of things to do, or find yourself at loss for how to expand an activity you meant to use with only a few students.

For example, if you have ten students and only four show up, you may find the lesson is over very quickly; if all your learners attend and you have become used to very small groups, then you may have to switch from a small group activity to one that can accommodate a far bigger number.

Paper-based games like a treasure hunt based on a text you've been using are easy to put together quickly. Just have students work on skimming for examples of grammar or facts that will answer a list of questions and award points to the students with the most correct. Alphabet War is a great card game, since it can be played in as many pairs as you need, and the only materials required are index cards and pencils. The game expands easily if you have students make their own decks as part of the activity. Most quiz games scale up or down to suit any size of class and are great for review. When you have very few students and you want to make reviewing what they have learned less like an interrogation, a game like Pyramid, where students play against the clock and gets points for how quickly they progress through each level, are ideal.

## Different Learning Styles

You come into class with a lesson on the present simple tense, or maybe with vocabulary or conversation exercises. You follow your textbook, give great examples to illustrate your points and have plenty of worksheets, but no matter what you do there are always two or three students who just don't get it. What's going wrong? Why aren't you getting through?

The answer may well lie in your students' learning styles. Learning styles have been studied for decades and there are several models that have been proposed by various researchers. While the finer distinctions are still debated, generally, most authorities in the field agree upon four basic learning styles: auditory, visual, kinaesthetic and tactile. There is a great deal of overlap between the last two styles, so they will be discussed together here.

In order to build your lessons around your students' learning styles, you need, firstly, to identify your main teaching style. Do you lecture, role-play, or use worksheets? Once you have figured this out, supplement it to fit your students' learning styles. Of course, in order to do this, you need materials and activities; you need flexibility, and – ideally – you want to add some fun. This is where the games come in. Their variety and the way in which games can be adapted to suit different ways of learning make them the perfect supplements to your usual teaching style.

### *Auditory learners*

Students who learn well through lectures, verbal explanations, tapes and oral instruction are generally classed as auditory learners. Games for this type of learner are mainly listening based and include those that involve repetition, dictation and listening for clues.

**Recitation games**    Recitation games involve students repeating language they have had demonstrated or written down for them. Telephone, Chants and Karaoke Night are good examples of these kinds of games. Karaoke Night works particularly well in Japan, where most students will be used to the idea of singing for workmates. It's not unusual to have a student ask you for help with preparing a song in English for a business party. If you are working with more conservative adults, variations of Chants, employing short, rhythmic dialogue and a metronome or hand clapping, can emphasize fluency.

**Listening games**    EFL students studying English in their own country often express concern that they only understand their teacher but no other native speakers. In the language classroom, work on listening skills by using recordings or videos with short dialogues. The game Vocabulary Scavenger Hunt, for example, involves trying to locate necessary vocabulary within multiple recordings at different listening stations. You could also adapt activities where students listen to a prepared recording while reading a transcript and fill in blanks with words they have just heard. Jigsaw Listening is also an excellent team-building game: teams send representatives to different listening stations and then try to reconstruct the story when all the listeners return to their groups. These kinds of games also help students learn how to make use of TV and radio broadcasts in English when studying on their own.

**Quiz and story-building games**     Quiz games like Jeopardy, Grammar Knock Out and listening memory games are great for auditory learners of any level since you can progress from asking basic questions about spelling and definitions to more challenging ones, such as how a word could be used in a sentence, an explanation of grammar rules or knowledge of cultural trivia.

Auditory learners also learn well from story- and sentence-building games like Mad Libs (either the store-bought variety or homemade), where students fill in words to make funny and nonsensical stories. These types of games require excellent listening skills, as the student keeps track of what will be required in his or her next turn, plus the game usually ends with a verbal recap of the finished story or sentence, allowing all students to check their understanding.

### *Visual learners*

Visual learners prefer to read silently and make good use of any illustrations that go with the text. They will generally prefer written instructions and will benefit from you acting out situations, or watching a demonstration, DVD or online clip. If you have a student who seems to retain what he or she reads better than what he or she hears, then that student is a perfect example of someone who prefers visual learning. There are many games that work with this kind of student, as well as assisting non-visual learners make the most of visual cues that can help them in using English.

**Board games**     There are plenty of commercial board games that can be used in the classroom, but it is possible to make your own. Folder games, which comprise laminated game boards stuck on to Manila folders with the pieces and cards needed to play stored in a bag stapled to the inside – can be made. These can be based on commercial boards and used to work on grammar, vocabulary, phonics and spelling.

Grammatical Chutes and Ladders, Parts of Speech Path Finding (based on the Candy Land Board) and A Day in the Life (based on the game Life), where students participate in mini role-plays generated by the roll of the die and scenario cards, are all fun to play. The boards should not be decorated in a childish way, as this will turn off your adult students, but they can still be colourful.

**Picture games**     These games include anything played with pictures as their main starting point. Playing games with picture flashcards or adapting Jeopardy using picture prompts are examples. Another, which is a lot of fun with advanced students, is picture captioning or comic strip re-writes. If you use comics from different countries, the class may become involved in some sophisticated discussions about what constitutes humour in different places.

Many students attain a certain level of advanced English and then plateau. One reason for this is that they have a difficult time taking their English outside of academic or basic survival situations. Studying humour through visual games can help to bridge that gap.

**Reading games**     Reading is an essential skill for all students and reading games will work especially well with visual learners. Reading Scavenger Hunts, using colour-coded pencils, involves students looking for particular parts of speech or vocabulary and teaches skimming as well as reviewing grammar and/or vocabulary. The game Ten Important Sentences with Watermelon, where teams send a representative to put sentences in order, helps with summarizing, working under pressure and team building. (The catch to this game is that the representative can only work on the problem for as long as he or she can keep repeating the word 'watermelon' without taking an extra breath.) This game has the added bonus of suiting tactile learners as well.

### *Tactile and kinaesthetic learners*

Tactile and kinaesthetic learners are often the students who just don't get what you're trying to explain in a traditional lecture or worksheet-based lesson. These learners take in information best when they use their whole bodies to complete exercises. Tactile learners are also physical learners, but they are more likely to learn things from model building and hands-on instruction. Interestingly, there was a study done in the late 1980s[1] that found the self-reported preference among English language learners for language lesson style was tactile/kinaesthetic by a wide margin. This just goes to show how important it is to try and integrate more physical and experiential elements into our English lessons.

---

[1] J.M. Reid (1987), 'The Learning Style Preferences of ESL Students', *TESOL Quarterly*, 21, pp. 87–111.

What makes a game kinaesthetic or tactile? Look for games that involve whole-body responses or have students touching and moving things around as part of the game activity. Games with these elements are associating physical activity and touch with specific meanings. They can be divided into three broad groups: touch games, spatial games and craft games.

**Touch games** The most common games involving touch are those based around having real items inside a bag, so that students have to touch the items and then perform certain tasks. These tasks are what differentiate the level of difficulty. The easiest version simply has students identify the objects that they touch in the bag. This is often a vocabulary game. To make it more difficult, students have to describe what they are feeling while the others try to guess what it is.

**Spatial games** These games involve rearranging items or people and can be both kinaesthetic and tactile. They include traditional games like charades and less traditional games like Population Punctuation, where all but one person in the group has a card with words or punctuation marks on it, and the learner who is 'it' tries to arrange the people (using as many as possible) at the front of the room so that the cards make a correctly punctuated sentence.

**Craft games** These include any game where students actually have to assemble something, like Lego Negotiations, where students negotiate with other teams for certain pieces to create a Lego creature according to the directions they've been given. This can also be done with homemade cardboard Tangrams (Chinese puzzles made of angled pieces of wood). Map drawing is another good example and can combine elements of auditory learning, since the teacher will tell students what to draw on their maps.

**Variety Brings Success**

Games are the easiest way to address different learning styles in the classroom. By putting students at ease and stimulating their senses, you create a wealth of learning opportunities.

Will paying attention to learning styles solve all your classroom problems? No, of course not. But using games to diversify your teaching style will allow you to reach more of your students more effectively than before. It will cut down on boredom, as games increase student interest, and will give students the chance to integrate different learning styles into their own style. Additionally, these opportunities aren't just for learning language – they can broaden the students' learning styles to include those that aren't their natural or first choice. Students will be doing more than just expanding their English when they play games. They will be expanding their minds.

## 2
## TEACHING TIPS

The games and activities in this book will allow your students a better chance of using English during your classes and to remember what they learn. Some games are disguised drills that give students frequent repetition when learning new vocabulary or a new grammatical structure. Other games encourage fluency. Although this book contains a mix of games that develop all learners' skills – reading, writing, listening and speaking – the main target is speaking. With beginners and lower intermediate students, use games in a greater portion of your class.

During the early stages of language learning plenty of drilling provides a solid foundation. Games allow you to do this in a pleasant way and students have to think about what they are saying rather than simply repeat things parrot fashion. With intermediate to advanced students, use concepts that develop fluency-based and more advanced games. Of course, you may also use the more basic games with higher-level groups, but much less often, and only when you wish to drill a particular grammatical point. This could be something that you have just introduced, or perhaps for revision purposes when you observe your students making frequent errors.

### Know Your Students' Goals

In your first lesson, survey the students. See what is most important to them and what they want to learn. It is highly likely that in most cases you will find that students want to learn to speak in English as a priority over reading and writing. Many adults will have already studied English in school, but still cannot talk freely or even understand much. You will probably find that students do not want to watch videos, read newspapers and fill in worksheets – they will most likely have done this before. In most cases, your students will want to spend much of the class time speaking and engaging in communication activities. That said, you may have a class that needs to be able to read or translate work-related documents, so surveying your learners regarding their motivation, needs and desires in English in the first lesson, if not before, is very important. However, if you have a class of multi-national beginners, you may well not get a chance to survey them before lessons start.

My inclination is always to focus on listening and speaking in class and (aside from written tests) save reading and writing for homework.

## Let Students Know Their Goals

Most adults have limited time to devote to projects such as learning English and want to feel their class time is filled to the brim. Therefore the key point is to make sure that you make games relevant to the language points and vocabulary you are teaching. It is vital to explain the exact purpose of a game or activity to students before starting. Is it designed to work with a specific grammatical point, or is it a fluency activity, and, if so, what is the focus? Is the activity designed to improve speaking skills through small talk, describing things, persuading people, storytelling, asking questions, or is it to encourage creative thinking?

## Using Drills

Beginners and intermediates need plenty of drills. Advanced students can benefit from these to iron out errors or to reinforce a new target structure. Use drills when you hear common errors in speaking fluency tasks or spot them in written homework. If a fluency task focuses on a particular grammatical structure or tense and you notice your students hesitating or making many errors, then stop – do some more drilling to give students a better grip of the language.

Drills are controlled speaking exercises that require students to repeat phrases or sentences without mistakes. In order for students to remember grammatical structures and use them during conversation, frequent out-loud repetition is necessary, and drills provide the opportunity. Otherwise, learners may simply copy things down in their notebooks without having a chance to absorb the language internally. Students may understand the target language if they hear or read it, but this does not mean that they can actually *use* it.

Drills can be done at normal pace first, in order to give students a chance to absorb the language. Then, play some games that encourage students to speak faster – such as Relay Race or Speed Drill – while drilling new language.

Parrot-fashion repetition is the most uninspiring type of teaching, so the game-playing suggestions in this book provide a more interesting context for drilling. They utilize elements such as team competitions, memory challenges, guessing games or use of required language. Any type of language can be drilled, from vocabulary to short sentences containing questions, or statements in any tense. The language being drilled should be new or slightly challenging for students, but not too complex. If a drill game does not work, it most likely means that the students are not ready to handle the language. Therefore, either simplify it, or use other listening games to prepare, and try again later in the same or next lesson.

## Using Fluency Activities: A Reason To Talk And A Reason To Listen

Most students will be prepared to speak about a given topic for the sole purpose of improving fluency. However, this can give rise to artificial conversations that quickly run dry. Communication is better when there are other reasons – in addition to using English – to talk. The activities in this book are designed to help in various ways, including introducing time limits and creating competition, for example by creating an information gap exercise wherein students have partial information and need to find out the rest, or where students need to persuade others to share their knowledge.

For example, rather than having students talk in pairs about their favourite home, let half the students be real estate agents and the other half be house buyers. The real estate agents have to convince the house buyers to buy their home and not someone else's. Allow a timeframe for conversation and then signal for the house buyers to move to a different agent. House buyers can visit several agents each before making their choice. See which agents made the most sales. While this is essentially the same speaking activity, the added twist makes it much more meaningful. Try to incorporate a sense of purpose to the communication in most, if not all, of your speaking fluency activities. (See the game Persuasion for more examples.)

Another important element of fluency activities is ensuring that the students have good reason to listen to each other. You might put students in pairs to discuss their favourite holiday destination or latest trip, but the students who are listening have no motivation to do so other than because they have been asked and out of politeness. However, if the students include three untrue facts in their description for the listener to identify by asking questions, suddenly the conversation takes on a whole new meaning.

Take care that the level of difficulty suits the class. Students can experience frustration when trying to debate topics for which they do not have the language.

**Accuracy Versus Fluency**

In general, there are two types of speaking activity: drills for accuracy and exercises for fluency. It is most important to ensure that the learners' language is correct when doing drills, but when doing fluency activities it is vital to let them talk freely, without you correcting errors. Listen in, and, when you hear a common mistake, return to a drill to iron it out. Equally, you cannot be a perfectionist and insist on everyone saying everything perfectly. The more advanced your students, the more errors they are likely to make. This is normal, as they are doing more talking! As long they can communicate, a few errors are acceptable. Plenty of British people make errors when speaking: for example, one of my friends recently commented 'There's hundreds of people in the street.' She meant, of course, 'There *are* hundreds of people in the street.' This is the kind of mistake that you hear often in spoken English, and if a British, postgraduate-educated person can make such an error, then give your learners a break – aim for great communication rather than perfect accuracy!

Many of the games in this book involve group work. This allows students to use the English language as much as possible during class. You cannot listen to everyone all the time, so do not try to be a control freak. Let students get on with it. Make sure you have properly introduced the target language first, though, using plenty of the listening activities games in this book. Follow these up with some controlled accuracy games, and then, in small groups, release your students to their own devices. These methods should improve the overall quality of their language. If you find many errors are being made, you know what you need to do: go back one step and drill some more, in a controlled environment.

**Storytelling**

In life, we tell stories all the time: what we did yesterday, what we are planning to do later, what the movie was like ... these are all stories of a sort. Storytelling aids fluency; additionally, it is generally more interesting than dry texts. Stories are dynamic, living things, and your students will be more motivated when talking about their own stories rather than about a distant, potentially out-of-date article in a textbook.

While some students may be confident and imaginative, you cannot rely on them all to come up with their own stories unaided. Provide something for them – pictures or words that they sequence, the first/last line of a story with some vocabulary to include – that will force their creativity. You may also ask students to talk about things that interest them and to retell familiar stories they know either from films they have seen, books they have read, or stories from childhood.

## Textbooks

Although you do not need to follow a textbook, doing so can reassure many learners, especially adults. Working through a textbook gives many a feeling of making progress, even if, in a worst-case scenario, this only involves the physical turning of the pages! Textbooks also give you, the teacher, a ready-made curriculum around which to base your lessons. Even if your students do not have a course textbook, get one for yourself, and use it as a basis for planning. You do not need to follow it slavishly, but you absolutely must supplement it with plenty of the games and speaking activities that you have at hand in this book, which can be applied in most cases to any language or grammar point. Textbooks are also extremely useful for assigning homework tasks.

## Classroom Discipline

Adults are usually highly motivated to learn. They are taking time out to do so, and time is precious. Therefore, unlike teaching children, you are unlikely to have any discipline problems in class. However, if you find students are chatting to each other instead of listening, then stop talking altogether and wait in silence. They will soon notice and stop talking without you having to say anything. If some students do not apply themselves, then really this is up to them – they are old enough to decide whether they want to waste their time. The most important thing is that they do not distract those who *do* want to learn.

If you have a problem with too much chatting, try the penalty jar idea. Every time a student tries to conduct an activity in a language other than English, or chats to another student, he or she has to put a ticket in the jar. At the end of the week, count up the tickets, and the learner with the lowest score wins. The students with the most tickets can have a penalty such as extra homework, or doing a forfeit such as preparing a presentation for the next lesson.

It may be that students are chatting because the pace of your lesson is too slow for them. Make sure you have all your materials ready so as to move seamlessly from one activity to another without delay. Downtime can immediately lead to talking amongst students, which in turn means that you have to work harder to regain their attention. Use some activities with time limits to increase the students' focus and put them under pressure to finish so that there is no time for chat. If you have multiple nationalities, put any students who speak the same first language into different groups and give them something to do if they finish first, such as a reading or writing task.

## Picture Or Word Flashcards?

Many games require picture or word flashcards. Picture cards are best for learning vocabulary, as students have to remember the words on their own, without the help of letters. They really need to be collated or bought, as it is best to avoid students spending valuable class time drawing pictures! However, if you are short of a picture or two, a quick sketch can save the day.

With more advanced students, word cards are fine, as you will be working on sentences and general speaking rather than simply learning vocabulary by this stage. Word cards are quick to handwrite or make on your PC – or just ask the students to write them out for you at the start of a class.

## What If A Game Flops?

One of the worse feelings in the world for teachers is watching an activity you've selected fall flat. It happens to the best teachers. How you handle this, though, is what makes the difference between success and failure in an overall lesson. How you handle such a situation will depend on exactly what is going wrong.

One possibility is that the students don't understand the language point of the activity. In this case, call a pause, review the grammar point, then start the activity again. It could be that you are going too fast for the students and they need to do more work before they can successfully perform the activity.

Another possibility is that students understand the language point but not the activity. In this case, step in and guide the students through it. If the task is a game, guide a few turns, and then let the students work independently.

Finally, it is possible that the point of the activity is not clear. Sometimes students are less interested in an activity because they think it is unimportant. The best way to get students to co-operate is to pause the activity and give concrete examples of what you are trying to accomplish.

## Preparation

Many teachers spend hours preparing for lessons. Why not ask students to contribute? For example, they could prepare for role-plays. Ask the students to come up with characters and roles in given settings for homework. In the next lesson, they can then act role-plays out in small groups. Give them time to rehearse and then ask each group to perform their work for the class.

If you look under Homework (p. xx), you will see a list of games for which students can prepare at home. Not only does this take a huge burden off the teacher, but it involves the students more in the task, meaning that they are more likely to be interested in it. If you mark any homework prior to a class, keep corrected versions in your materials for use with a different group in the future.

In general, prepare thoroughly, and if necessary rehearse the lesson. This will make you feel more confident. Test out your ideas on a colleague if you are unsure. Always prepare more than you plan to use, and if you have two or three quick vocabulary or grammar games from this book on standby then you will always have something on which to fall back.

Make sure to keep a list of common errors that your class makes. If you have spare time, go over them frequently, using short grammar games. Keep these activities up your sleeve if you have a blank, if you don't know what to do because only half the students have turned up, you finish early, or you stop an activity because it seems not to be working.

At first, you will take longer to prepare for lessons, but as you implement more and more of the activities in this book your preparation time will be cut right down and your lessons will get better and better.

## Encourage Your Students, And Be Kind To Yourself!

It is normal to feel nervous before your first class, sometimes before many classes. However, there is no point in undermining yourself: don't listen to the inner voice of doubt, but to the voice that told you to become a teacher, and remember why you made that choice. As long as your English is better than your students' and you have great range of teaching tools at your disposal, then you are of service to them. You do not have to understand every aspect of English grammar either, but *do* have an excellent reference book in which to look things up, and which helps you to answer questions. Many native English speakers often have to look things up in grammar books!

After a lesson, think about it briefly, and learn from what worked and what did not. A lesson is never a failure – it is always a learning experience. If you are enjoying your classes, then the likelihood is that so are your students!

Be friendly, enthusiastic, encouraging, and smile at your group. It is important that you believe in them and in their capacity to learn. Never demean a student or imply he or she is stupid. People flourish when they feel nurtured and safe. Destructive criticism is a killer, and this includes you beating yourself up mentally and worrying about your classes.

Most adults feel self-conscious about the idea of speaking a foreign language, so in the first lessons be particularly encouraging and gentle on your learners. Your reassuring attitude will allow their confidence and abilities to grow.

# PART 2

## GAMES A–B

Use the detailed index above to select games.

### A Day In The Life

| | |
|---|---|
| Category | Speaking drill or speaking fluency |
| Group size | Any, with students in small groups |
| Level | All levels |
| Preparation | Create your own board, or use the example provided in the downloadable Appendix |
| Materials | See Appendix for two boards and card sets plus one blank set ready to fill in; a folder or card for the board; markers to draw the board and decorate it; buttons or coins as game pieces; a die; 30 index cards |

This activity is based on the board game Game of Life. The board can be drawn on the inside of a folder and laminated; the cards and die can be kept in clear bags stapled to the folder.

The example provided is A4 size (8.5 x 11 inches), which you could print on to card; alternatively, you could print it on to paper and then stick it to a larger piece of card. Three boards are provided: one has adult activities filled in and role-play cards to go with them; one is for teens; finally, there is a blank template for you to fill in as best suits your needs. For example, to make a very easy version, draw pictures of objects that students can name and then make sentences using the nouns. To drill specific grammar, ask all questions in a specific tense, or adapt the game to use target language. For general fluency, use a mixture of tenses and scenarios, as shown in the examples provided.

**Preparation**  This game takes around 60 to 90 minutes to make, or use the pre-prepared one in the downloadable Appendix. Once completed, you only have to update the role-play cards. You will need to make a list of things people do during a normal day, or use the one provided in the downloadable Appendix: get up, brush teeth, go to school/work, have lunch, meet friends, ask a person out on a date, etc. The list should be age appropriate for your students. A good way to generate it is to have a brainstorming session with your students during a previous lesson.

Once you have your list, draw a path with 24 spaces on the board (a space for every hour of the day). Make the path twisty so that it takes up the space on the board, but remember to leave enough room in which to write. Choose three spaces and write 'Oh yeah!' in them; in another three write 'Oh no!'

To complete the remaining squares you need to go the list of everyday actions and connect them, in the order in which they would happen during a real day, to conversational situations, for example: 'You have to get up – tell the person waking you that you want to sleep for another five minutes.'

On 15 index cards, write 'Oh yeah!' on one side and various lucky events on the other side, alongside instructions that allow the player to move up the path. For example, 'Win the lottery – tell the person next to you and then skip ahead three spaces!' On the other 15 cards, write 'Oh no!' on one side and bad luck events on the other. These cards could cause the player to move back down the path – for example, 'You've had a car accident. Convince the police officer sitting to your left that it wasn't your fault. If he/she doesn't believe you, go back two spaces.'

The best way in which to find out what 'good' and 'bad' events would appeal to your students is to ask each class member to write down a few for homework.

For beginners, make the 'Oh yeah!' and 'Oh no!' cards very simple – for example, giving vocabulary or making a short sentence including a certain word. You can indicate whether a player needs to move forwards or backwards by including +2, -1 and so on. For intermediates and up, use such scenarios as described above to create the need for conversation.

Everyone rolls the die and the lowest roll goes first. The players take turns to roll and move their pieces, following the instructions on the space in which they land. The winner is the first player to make it to the end.

## Alibi

| Category | Step 5 speaking fluency |
| --- | --- |
| Group size | Any |

| Level | Lower intermediate to advanced |
|---|---|
| Preparation | Optional descriptions of alibis to give to students – see Appendix |
| Materials | None obligatory, but useful for lower intermediates |

**How to play**       Tell the class that a crime has been committed and give a description of someone who was spotted at the scene (one of the class members). That person goes out of the room or to a corner with a few other students to establish an alibi, i.e. to discuss where he or she was and what he or she was doing at that time.

While this is happening, the other students are divided into groups and prepare questions to ask the suspect and his or her friends. When a few minutes are up, the suspect group divides up, one suspect per group of questioners. Allow two minutes' question time only before the suspects rotate around the class. The class then decides if the person is guilty or not, depending on how many discrepancies they find in the details of the alibi given.

This game gets better when re-played and students are able to come up with more questions to snare the suspect. Use it two or three times over a term and make sure different students are chosen for the suspect group.

With lower intermediates – especially the first time you play – you might want to provide pre-prepared alibis and questions.

- Examples for the suspects: 'I was at my friend Dave's house.' 'We went for a pizza and met up with friends.' 'I had pepperoni pizza and a Coke.'

- Examples for the questioners: 'Where were you?' 'What were you doing at the time?' 'Then what did you do?' 'Did you eat anything?' 'What were you wearing?' 'Was Dave's mother there?'

**Alphabet Games**

*Alphabet A – Listening*

| Category | Step 1 listening drill – alphabet |
|---|---|
| Group size | Any |
| Level | Beginner |
| Materials | Letters of the alphabet from Scrabble sets/on paper |
| Preparation | None |

While it may seem logical to start a beginners' group by teaching the alphabet, it is more rewarding for students to start with greetings, nouns and simple sentences, which give them the impression they are getting somewhere fast. The letters of the alphabet can be introduced early, a few letters at a time.

**How to play**     Let students work individually, in pairs or small groups, as you prefer, or divide the class into small groups of two to four per team. Give each group a pile of letters and spell out a word. The students take the relevant letters from the pile and form the word on their tables.

To start, give out different letter combinations, such as all the consonants and the vowel a, and suggest easy words such as pat, cat, fat etc. In round two, you could use the same combinations of consonants but substitute a for i to create words such as fit, bit and pit. (It is OK if students do not understand all the words they make. The important thing is that they become familiar with the sounds of the alphabet.)

**Materials**     If you do not have the necessary materials, ask students to make their own letters, which you can dictate to them or which they can copy from the board. Using letters on card, scrabble letters or (even better) fridge magnet letters helps the kinaesthetic and tactile learners and improves their chances of remembering the lesson subsequently.

## Alphabet B – Speaking

| | |
|---|---|
| Category | Step 2 speaking drill – alphabet and vocabulary |
| Group size | Small to medium-sized groups divided into teams |
| Level | Beginner to intermediate |
| Materials | None |
| Preparation | None |

**How to play**     You or a class member spell a word out loud (do not write it down) to one team, such as c–a–t. The team has three seconds to call out the word you spelled, in this case 'cat'. If the team has not named the word within the three seconds, other students are free to call out the word to win a point for their team (if you are keeping score).

To encourage all students to use the vocabulary, have a rule where, as well as the person who guesses it first, the whole team must call out the word within the three-second limit. Although the quickest students

33

will still name the word first, the rest of the team must be listening and ready to chime in before the three seconds are up in order for the team to win its point. Alternatively, allow each team member one turn at calling out the word, or allow team members to whisper the answer to those who have not yet had a turn at calling out the word.

For more advanced students, use words that are harder to spell, or those with silent letters.

## Alphabet War

| | |
|---|---|
| Category | Step 2 speaking drill – alphabet and vocabulary |
| Group size | Any class size, working in pairs or small groups |
| Level | Beginner to intermediate |
| Materials | Letters – see printable appendix; 26 index cards for each student; markers – a different colour for each person is ideal |
| Preparation | Cut out and distribute card |

This game is based on the traditional card game War. It provides a fun way to work on letters and sounds.

**Preparation**    Print the Alphabet War cards found in the downloadable Appendix, one set per pair or small group of students. Paper is fine, though card is nicer for players to manipulate. Give each student 26 cards and have them write the alphabet (specifying whether they need to use capitals or lower-case letters) out with the marker, one letter per card.

**How to play**    Pair up the students, or play in very small groups. Then have students shuffle their decks. Students lay down their top cards and compare them. The student with the letter closest to A wins the match and takes both cards. This helps students to learn alphabetical order. When the deck has been used up, the players pick up the cards they have won, shuffle them and start again. If time is a concern, limit the game to three rounds – the player with the most cards at the end wins.

### Variation

As an optional rule, in order to take the cards, the winning player has to give the pronunciation of the letter and a word that has the letter in it, or he or she forfeits the cards to the other player.

## Anagrams

| | |
|---|---|
| Category | Spelling |
| Group size | Divide the class into pairs or very small groups |
| Level | Beginner to advanced |
| Materials | Class board; optional use of individual letters such as Scrabble sets or letter flashcards – the letters from Alphabet War (see Appendix) could be used |
| Preparation | Decide on the words or sentences to be deciphered |

**How to play**  Write words in a jumble on the board, such as 'l e p e h n t a' for 'elephant'. Either use words that are in the same vocabulary family, such as food words or professions, or, if using unrelated words, give a clue with every set of letters.

Divide the class into teams and give each team a name, such as a colour. On your signal, the players race to make up the words. The first one to decipher a word writes it up on the board with the team name next to it. You may like to suggest that there is no need to solve the anagrams in the order they appear – teams can pick any word from the list to decipher. If it is evident that some teams are far quicker than the others, swap the students around so the talent is evenly spread about the classroom.

For small groups of students it is more fun to play this game with real letters from Scrabble games or letter flashcards. Give each group a pile of letters. Call out the letters of a word in a jumbled order and give a time limit for the word to be deciphered. The first to work out his or her word writes it up on the board. At this point, give out the next set of letter to decipher.

Another variation is to give each team a big pile of letters containing several words. On the board, have either pictures or clues, or deciphering the vocabulary may be too difficult. On your signal, each team works together to form all the words from the pile.

### *Variations*

- Gap fill

Write or read out a sentence including a gap. Provide the missing word in jumbled form. For example:

Do you _____ (k i e l) butter?
Answer: like

- Small group

Another fun way to play if you have a small group is to give each player or team a buzzer. The bells you often find on hotel receptions are good for this purpose. Write the scrambled letters of a word on the board. All players try to figure out the word (give them clues if necessary), and as soon as a player knows the answer he or she hits the buzzer to get a point for the team if correct. Do not deduct points for wrong answers so as not to discourage people from trying, but do deduct a point for ringing the bell with no answer ready.

If you have only two or three teams, give them each a certain amount of time (say 15 seconds) to figure out a word, after which the round is open to the buzzers of the other teams. If necessary, rig the game to keep all the teams' scores very close together, for example by giving easier words to a team that is lagging behind.

**Additional materials**     Use plastic Ziploc bags (like freezer or sandwich bags) to transport sets of letters without loss. Alternatively, dispense altogether with letters, and write the words in a jumble on the board. The students can decipher them in their heads, or using pen and paper.

## Battleships

| Category | Step 2 or 5 – may be used for speaking drills or for fluency |
|---|---|
| Group size | Two people, or two teams – teams should be three people per team or fewer |
| Level | Beginner to advanced |
| Materials | 10 x 100-square grids (example grids are included in the downloadable Appendix); folders, books or similar to act as screens between players |
| Preparation | Students prepare game grids in or before class |

This game is based on a popular American board game called Battleships. It is very quick to prepare before class, but there needs to be time in class to create the grids, as this is part of the vocabulary work. The purposes of this exercise include review of previously taught vocabulary, giving descriptions and development of memory, logic, and strategy.

Additional preparation time is minimal: all you need is to prepare a 10 x 10-squares grid, with squares big enough to mark within clearly, and run off enough copies for each student or team to have two. See the downloadable Appendix for blank and ready-made grids.

**How to play**   In class, have each player or team take two grids. They will work with their opposing team and fill out all the grids so that they are identical. On the vertical axis of the grid (the y-axis), have them list the alphabet – A, B, C, D, and so on, or list a letters in random order, as you prefer. On the horizontal axis (the x-axis), list vocabulary categories that you want to review (animals, food, jobs, etc.). Then have students fill in the grid. For example, looking at the grid, C–Clothes might have 'coat', or 'cap' written in the box; G–Food might have 'goat's cheese' or 'grapes'.

For beginners, use the simpler version with letters and categories. See the Appendix for an example of each.

Example of an intermediate- to advanced-level Battleships grid.

| | Food | Clothes | Country | Place | Adjective | Verb | Adverb | Sport | Profession | Animal |
|---|---|---|---|---|---|---|---|---|---|---|
| A | Apple | Anorak | America | Airport | Angry | To | Angrily | Archery | Actor | Ant |
| B | Bread | Boots | Britain | Bank | Big | To beat | Badly | Bowling | Banker | Bat |
| C | Coconut | Cap | Chad | Cinema | Cold | To count | Creepily | Cycling | Chiropractor | Cat |
| D | Donut | Dress | Denmark | Dentist | Dark | To die | Doggedly | Darts | Dentist | Dog |
| G | Goat's cheese | Gloves | Ghana | Garage | Great | To go | Gladly | Gymnastics | Gardener | Goat |
| H | Hummus | Hat | Haiti | Home | Happy | To have | Happily | Hiking | Hairdresser | Hippo |
| M | Meat | Mittens | Mexico | Meadow | Mighty | | Mildly | ? | Medic | Monkey |
| R | Rice | Raincoat | Russia | Room | Red | To risk | Rapidly | Rugby | ? | Rat |
| S | Salad | Socks | Spain | Shop | Silly | To see | Stupidly | Skating | Secretary | Snake |
| T | Toast | Tie | Trinidad | Town | Tight | To take | Timidly | ? | Typist | Tiger |

If students are stuck on a square, for example if they cannot think of an item of clothing beginning with the letter 'G', then they can choose to leave that square blank. However, battleships may not be placed in a blank square.

If students work together to complete a grid for homework, then the internet is a fantastic tool. For example, simply searching 'list of countries' will yield a result, allowing students to fill in their grids easily rather than agonizing over them. Placing students into groups for the creation of grids will help enormously, as they will pool knowledge and ideas. There should be no penalties for using the Internet or dictionaries as long as students know what a word means, or where a country is.

Once the grids are filled out, each player or team takes two and marks one as MINE (or OURS) and the other as HIS (or HERS, or THEIRS) and the separating screens are set up. The players then draw their battleships on the grids. The ships may be placed horizontally or vertically, but not diagonally. Students should draw ships to take up the following spaces: one that covers three spaces, two that cover two spaces, and three that cover one space. The object of the game is to find and destroy the opponent's ships.

**How to play**          Once ships are drawn, play begins. The first player to have a turn guesses the location of the opponent's ship, and describes the vocabulary item that is in the square (for example, saying 'Something you drive with four wheels' would indicate 'car', which could be a vocabulary item under a category C–Machines). Beginners playing may simply name items or drill basic sentences such as 'I like cars' or 'I can drive a car' and so on. Intermediates and above can be given specific structures or tenses to drill, or the game can be used for speaking fluency.

If there is a ship in the square guessed, the opponent says 'Hit.' If the ship is completely hit, then the opponent must say 'Hit and sunk.' If there is nothing in the square, then the opponent says 'Miss.' Whatever the opponent says, the player marks the grid labelled 'his', 'hers' or 'theirs' with the opponent's response.

If the player scored a hit, he or she gets another turn; if a miss, the turn goes to the opponent. The game carries on until the one player or team has sunk all of the opponent's ships.

Keep the grids and type them up so that you have a supply to use in future, but minus the class preparation time. Consider allowing dictionaries, both for the creation of grids and when using grids prepared by other students.

I gave all students a blank school timetable. Then I asked them to put one English battleship of four blocks, two Maths battleships of three blocks, three Science battleships of two blocks and four History battleships of one block. Then they added other activities. With their timetables filled in, I divided them into pairs, and they had to find their partner's ships by asking, for example, 'What do you do/study at 10 o'clock on Tuesday?'

## Bingo

| Category | Step 1 listening drill |
|---|---|
| Group size | Any |
| Level | Beginner |
| Materials | Bingo sets |
| Preparation | None, if students make bingo sets on the spot, as described below |

**How to play**   The students each have a different card with several numbers on. The teacher calls out the numbers randomly and the students circle the numbers on their cards when they are called. When a student has circled all the numbers, he or she says 'Bingo!' and the game has finished. You can also play with dates, vocabulary and with sentences.

Use this game with any group size. No materials are needed: have, for example, each class member write down four numbers between 1 and 10. You then randomly call out the numbers 1 to 10, and whenever a player has a number you call he or she circles it until all four numbers are circled. Continue until you have a winner, or until everyone has finished, or anything in between. Bingo games work for any sequences of numbers, including  10, 20, 30, 40 etc., or 100, 200, 300, etc.

Use the same methods for nouns. Write or show pictures of a selection of nouns, and let students select three or four of these. They can either sketch rapidly or write down the words, thus making a bingo card for the game. Use ready-made bingo cards if you have them, but they are not obligatory.

**Language ideas**        Bingo is a good game to use at an early stage of presenting language as it exposes the players to frequent repetition of new vocabulary or language. With beginners, limit yourself to simply naming the items – 'car', 'dress', 'swimming pool', 'house'. You can then add more detail: 'red dress', 'old house', 'green car'. Expose your players to more vocabulary still by adding more description – 'a beautiful red dress', 'a green sports car' – and introduce them to grammatical structures such as 'I wish I had a green car.' Students could also ask questions in unison, such as, 'How are we going to the beach?' You reply, 'We are going by car.'

As the one making the calls, you need a system in place to ensure you call each picture once, such as writing all the words on a list and ticking them off as you call them.

Forming sentences with a chosen word will encourage attentive listening. If you are playing Bingo with all new words, then form sentences with structures the class already knows. However, if you are using Bingo to review vocabulary, then introduce a new grammatical structure through the game so that students hear it repeatedly.

As a final point, I have heard of teachers playing bingo with small change. I do not recommend this, as it turns it into a gambling game, which can clash with certain cultures. Also, there is no reason why the teacher should spend his or her own money in an attempt to bribe the class to be interested! Asking students to chip in money could also arouse resentment.

## Blow Your House Down

| | |
|---|---|
| Category | Step 2 speaking drill |
| Group Size | 2 to 20 students, or larger numbers they can work in groups |
| Level | Beginner to lower intermediates |
| Materials | Pictures or word flashcards |
| Preparation | None |

Students are divided into two teams with a maximum of 10 students per team, or the game will become boring. If you have more than 20 students, let games run simultaneously.

A student comes up to the front and picks a card from a pile. The student then names the vocabulary shown on the card, or makes a sentence or question as required by you. Consider using verbs or other words, not just nouns. If successful, the student can draw the first line of a house on the board. (Provide a model that can be copied – I suggest a simple house than can be drawn in six strokes.) If incorrect, the student cannot contribute to the team's house. Team 2 decides if the sentence is correct. If Team 2 is wrong, their house is blown down. Repeat with a member from Team 2. If a team member makes a mistake, their house is blown down. The winner is the team that 'builds' their six-line house first.

This can also be a collaborative game, where team members correct their own sentences to save having the team house blown down. Such a useful variant empowers the whole team and keeps all students involved.

To keep the pace flowing, allow students to come up and turn over their card in advance of their turn so that there is absolutely no delay between students making their sentences. Team B's student can be thinking up his or her sentence while team A's is writing/saying his or hers and drawing the house. This will make the best use of time and prevent students from sitting around waiting while someone scratches his or her head and tries to come up with an answer. It also takes the pressure off the student whose turn it is, which may be appreciated. If a student does not like being put on the spot in this way, send that student up in a pair.

For mixed-ability classes, let the stronger students arbitrate a group, referring to the teacher if in doubt over a particular sentence.

## Boggle

| Category | Spelling |
|---|---|
| Group size | Class work in small groups or individually |
| Level | All, but better for intermediates and upwards |
| Materials | Class board |
| Preparation | Decide on your Boggle grids in advance |

**How to play** Ideally, prepare the board in advance by drawing five 3 x 3 grids on the board, as below. If possible, use existing nine-letter words to fill out the grids, but jumble up the letters, as in the original Boggle game.

Students could work individually or in small groups of two or three. Allow two minutes for the players to write down as many words as they can find in the given letters. When you say 'Stop' everyone moves on to the next grid. Allow another two minutes for the next grid and so on until you have done them all. (Of course, you can just use one or two grids if this is going to take too long!)

When reviewing, take each set of letters in turn and let each group tell you its words. The groups could also swap over their answers with another group. Award points as you see fit. For example, teams get 1 point for a valid word, and 3 points if they discovered the original nine-letter word. Alternatively, only award points for words that no other teams have found. Continue through the answers, taking each set of letters in turn.

Here is an example of a grid using the word 'adventure', which is a good choice as it has several vowels.

| a | u | e |
|---|---|---|
| n | t | d |
| r | v | e |

41

Other than adventure, words that can be found in this grid are tune, dune, rune, reed, den, dent, vent, rent, runt, date, rate, tread, dean, teen, never, net, tan, van, deer, dear, read, deed, veer, near, tar, dart, ate, tuna, urn, turn, Ned, Ted, vet, drat, nave, Dave, rave, raved, tat, due, rant, neat, tee, red, ran, run, rat, van, TV, tea, eat, ten ... That's 52, and there are doubtless more. Many of these words are advanced vocabulary, but beginners might find red, ran, run, rat, van, TV, tea, eat and ten. It's up to you whether you allow names/proper nouns or not.

It does not matter if the letters of the word do not make a 9 x 9 square grid. Here are some examples of useful words to try on your students: manufacture, introduction, intermediate, brainstorm, intelligence, fabrication, treadmill and recommendation.

## Brainstorm And Rhyming Brainstorm

| Category | Step 2 speaking drill |
|---|---|
| Group size | 2 players up to a class of 30 |
| Level | Lower intermediate to advanced |
| Materials | Stopwatch/timer |
| Preparation | Decide on the vocabulary themes you will use |

**How to play**  Give each player or team 30 seconds to come up with as many words as possible in a given category. All the players in the team call out words as and when they think of them, in free-for-all style. Designate one student for each team to count up the words while you man the stopwatch. To prevent one student from taking over the whole game, have a quota of two words per team member, after which a team member who has used up his or her quota can whisper additional words to a teammate.

Once the 30 seconds are up, the floor opens to all other teams who have a chance to earn points if they can name any other vocabulary that has not yet been mentioned. You then give the next team a new theme for a 30-second brainstorm. By all means, give 15 or 20 seconds if this is more appropriate to the level of your class, and always err on the side of not giving enough time to keep up the adrenalin and the element of fun.

Aside from a vocabulary revision brainstorming activity, require instead that participants use sentences. You may like to drill a target structure such as 'I should have seen ...' Combine this with a vocabulary theme such as famous people, musicians or animals. Rather than just calling out single words, students now call out the designated sentence with a different conclusion each time.

Categories to use can include professions, sports, cartoon characters, musicians, famous people, household objects, furniture, body parts, clothing, hobbies, types of transport, musical instruments, animals, types of food, toys, jobs, countries, favourite characters, nouns from nature, nouns from a specific place such as a hospital or school, things you do at school, things you do in a hot place, a cold place, at a zoo and so on.

### *Variations*

An advanced version of this game requires you to give a category and a letter of the alphabet. So you might say Animals and B – the class calls out bull, bear, bat, beaver, badger, bird, bee, beetle or bug. This is much, much harder. Allow a minute for each round or the game may drag.

For Rhyming Brainstorm, which is more challenging, have your players get together in teams and write down all the words they can think of that rhyme with each other, or that have a certain spelling pattern. For example, ask them to write down all the words that rhyme with the sound 'a', as in lay. Intermediates might come up with words such as day, say, play, clay, pay, tray, bay, Fay, gay, hay, May or may, way, pray. Advanced players might come up with words such as weigh, daily, neigh, fray, play, delay, jay, display, flay.

Give the teams a limited time of two minutes to write down their words before holding a play off, where each team takes it in turns to call out one of their words. If a word has already been said, it cannot be used again, and it must be crossed off the list.

When a team has no more words to offer, it is out, and the remaining teams keep batting words backwards and forwards between themselves until only one team is left. The play off must be fast paced with a four-second timeframe for a team to return a word, or the team misses a go. Adapt the number of seconds as necessary, but keep an eye on the pace – the sense of urgency is what makes this game fun.

### Buddy Reading

| | |
|---|---|
| Category | Reading out loud and listening |
| Group size | Any working in pairs |
| Level | Beginner to advanced; good for multilevel classrooms |
| Materials | Texts to read |
| Preparation | None |

Buddy reading involves one student reading and the 'buddy' helping to make sure that the reader is pronouncing the words correctly. The buddy also asks questions after the reading to check comprehension.

You will need to model buddy reading for the group first, but with adults this is often a very easy multi-level activity for them to pick up since it is similar to studying together outside of class. Higher-level students are able to monitor lower-level students, and, interestingly, having lower-level students monitoring higher-level students often works too as the higher-level students become more aware of embedded errors that they are making.

## Build a Sentence

| | |
|---|---|
| Category | Step 3 reading, grammar |
| Group size | Divide class into groups of four |
| Level | Fully flexible |
| Materials | Sets of cards are provided in the Appendix – use at least four per student; four boxes, bags or hats to hold the cards; pen and paper or a chalk/white board |
| Preparation | Play with the set provided in the Appendix, or you may have the students prepare in the lesson |

Take four cards at a time and write a one word on each: a noun, a verb, an adjective and an adverb. Continue until you have at least 20 cards. Sort the cards so that all the nouns, verbs, adjectives and adverbs are in their own containers.

Play for 10–30 minutes, or as long as there is interest.

**How to play**    This is a co-operative game. Break your class up into teams (ideally of four) and give each team its own set of cards. You should play one or two rounds as a class in order to give everyone an idea of how play progresses. Talking is only allowed in English when discussing possible sentences, and any team caught using a first language incurs a penalty point.

Assign each member of the team a task: recorder (writes the sentence down), timekeeper, reader and arranger. If there are more team members than jobs, then rotate the jobs each round. The reader pulls one card from a box and reads it aloud. Let's say the word is 'cat'.

The timekeeper starts the clock, and the team has one minute to think of a sentence with 'cat' in. The students think of 'I have a cat.' The recorder writes it down. The group now has three minutes to continue drawing one card each from any of the boxes in turn and building up their sentence.

The reader reads each card aloud and the team decides where to put it in the sentence, or if they can't use it. So, for example, the second word drawn might be the verb 'see'. Students think up and write down the sentence 'I see a cat.' The third word drawn is 'blue'. Students write down 'I see a blue cat.' If they can't use a card, it goes on the discard pile. Students get a point for every card they use correctly, and lose a point for every card they don't use.

A, the, and, but, or and other prepositions are free words – there are no points for using them, but students don't need to draw a card for them either. You don't have to keep score unless you are playing teams against each other. Sentences do not have to make perfect sense – sometimes they will be funny and surreal – but they do have to be grammatically correct.

GAMES C–D

## Call My Bluff

| | |
|---|---|
| Category | Step 5 speaking fluency |
| Level | Beginner to advanced |
| Group size | Any |
| Materials | Optional; students can prepare descriptions for homework or in class |
| Preparation | Prepare a description with false elements about yourself to use as a demonstration |

You may need to demonstrate this task first in class and then ask students to prepare as homework, or allow a few minutes in class for students to consider what they will say about themselves. Then have a student stand up and make three statements about him or herself, two true and one false. The class decides which fact is untrue. Do this a couple of times in front of the whole class and then split into small groups to continue the activity.

Other topics to use for beginners are what they did at the weekend. Students prepare a description of what they did at the weekend and include three untrue facts. The other students try to guess what these untrue facts are, either by pure guesswork or by asking additional questions about the weekend to the student (a more advanced activity).

Describing anything that has taken place, such as a previous holiday or job, will elicit use of the past tense. Describing anything in the future, such as what students intend to do after class, or during the next holiday period, will drill the future. Describing what they would do if they lived in another country or if they could do anything they liked will work on the conditional, and so on. Set your scenario according to the language you wish to focus on.

With beginners and lower intermediate students it is best if students prepare their descriptions for homework prior to the class and you mark them. This way, students will find the activity easier, and there will be more fluent speaking taking place.

## *Variations*

One variant is for students to prepare information what they really intend to do at the weekend, or did last weekend, and when they arrive in class give out two or three alternative activities per student that they must slip into their descriptions. The partner or class must find out through questions which activities have been added. This is best for lower intermediates and upwards rather than beginners.

## Call My Bluff Definitions

| Category | Writing, reading; from simple vocabulary definitions to enriching knowledge of English through metaphors |
|---|---|
| Level | Beginner to advanced |
| Group size | Any |
| Materials | See Metaphors for some examples |
| Preparation | Students prepare definitions for homework |

**Vocabulary version**     Students prepare three definitions of a word that they look up in the dictionary, one true and two false. The class must listen to the definitions and decide which are false.

Once students have heard all three definitions, have them stand at their desks and listen as the definitions are read out again. This time, students sit down if they think a definition is false and stay standing if they think it is true. This way, it is easy to see who is correct. Tell those students who were correct to award themselves a point. Ideally, give the preparation task as homework so as not to use class time for research. You could have a choice of more possible answers for variety, but having one true and two false is best for beginners.

**Metaphors, idioms or sayings version**     Idioms    are    words, phrases or expressions that cannot be taken literally. In other words, when used in everyday language, they have a meaning other than the basic one you would find in the dictionary. Every language has its own idioms. Learning them makes understanding and using a language a lot easier and more fun! They are best tackled with advanced or higher-level intermediate groups.

For example, 'break a leg' is a common English idiom. The literal meaning is 'I command you to break a bone in your leg.' The idiomatic meaning is 'Do your best.' Often, actors tell each other to 'break a leg' before they go out on stage to perform.

Students choose a metaphor or expression and give three definitions of the meaning, two fake and one true. This is an enriching exercise. Alternatively, distribute metaphors or expressions, one or two per student, and let them research the meanings for homework. More advanced students could be given free rein to find their own metaphors or expressions.

## Chants

| | |
|---|---|
| Category | Step 5 fluency activity |
| Level | Beginner to intermediate |
| Group size | Divide a large class into small groups |
| Materials | Sentences, songs or a reading passage, a metronome is optional |
| Preparation | None |

Give students short dialogues, lyrics from songs or any written material that you want to work with. Students are to read out their text with a rhythm in the background. Use a metronome if you have one, or have the class or a partner clapping rhythmically as the beat. Students are free to fit the text into the beat as best they can. Some students who are musical will do this well naturally and for others it will be harder. If you try this yourself first you will see that it is excellent for encouraging fluency, as often one is obliged to run many words together quickly to fit into a beat.

The pace of the beat should not be too fast. One beat per second is quite slow, and you could use this for beginners. Here are some examples of how the first words of this game's explanation can be read. The syllable in bold indicates where the beat falls, which is when the other students clap.

Give—stu—dents—short—di—a—logues

This is one syllable per beat. You don't want this, as it is dreary and too slow.

**Give**—**stu**-dents—**short**—**di**-a-logues

This is much better, and students have to say the word 'dialogues' quite quickly to fit it into the beat.

Give—**stu**—dents—short—**di-a**-logues [pause for comma]
**ly**—rics—from—**songs**

This is far more musical – the student has started on the upbeat with 'Give'.

Here is an extended example for those of you who may still be unsure. Clap a steady beat and say the words below with an accent on the syllable in bold, which you say at the same time as the clap. The other syllables fit rhythmically into the space between claps.

Give **stu**dents short **di**alogues, **ly**rics from **songs** or **any writ**ten ma**ter**ial that **you** want to **work** with. **Students clap** on **words** in **bold** and **read** out the **text** with a **rhythm** in the **back**ground.

If you are not musical and you do not know what an upbeat or triplet is, don't worry – you do not need to know about these things! Experiment beforehand with saying some text in different rhythms to a beat so that your demonstration is convincing. Everyone benefits from this activity, whether musical or not!

## Charades

| Category | Step 2 speaking fluency |
|---|---|
| Group size | Best with small groups |
| Level | Intermediate |
| Materials | None |
| Preparation | Think up some good film and book titles relevant to your students to suggest during the game (for ideas, use the internet) |

**How to play**   One person mimes a book, a song or a film title by acting out each word or miming the idea expressed in the whole title. Those watching have to guess the book, song or film.

The player miming is not allowed to speak at all and starts by indicating if he or she is miming a book (pretend to open a book), a song (pretend to sing), or a film (pretend to hold a movie camera). The other players respond to the mime by calling out the answer, for example, 'It's a film' or/and 'It's a book.' The player miming then specifies how many words are in the title by holding up the relevant number of fingers, and the other players respond, for example, 'Five words.'

The player miming can then either act out the whole title, or choose to act out one of the words; for example, he or she might hold up five fingers and the audience responds with 'Fifth word.' The actor mimes working in a factory until someone guesses 'factory' correctly. Next he or she might hold up two fingers for the second word and indicate that this is a little word by holding thumb and forefinger close together, as if holding a small object between them. The audience responds with 'a', 'the', 'it', 'an' and so on until someone says 'and', which is the correct word in this mime. So far we have 'and' and 'factory' – in this case, the book and film is *Charlie and the Chocolate Factory*.

Players can also mime syllables of words. For example, hold up two fingers for second word, and then place one finger on your forearm to indicate first syllable. Then mime making a pot on a wheel to get the first syllable 'pot' of the word Potter for a Harry Potter film or book. In addition to syllables, one can also mime things that sound like the word to be guessed. The person miming holds a hand up to his or her ear and the players respond with 'sounds like ...' One might mime 'carry', which sounds like Harry.

**Comparatives Get In Order**

| | |
|---|---|
| Category | Step 2 speaking drill |
| Level | Beginner to Intermediate |
| Group size | Best for smaller groups, or split the class |
| Materials | None |
| Preparation | Decide on the themes students will use to put themselves in order |

All students stand up and put themselves in order to review comparatives. Example orders include tallest to shortest, order of birthdays, distance lived from class, number of years they have been learning English, number of times they have visited a certain place, number of brothers and sisters, number of jobs they have held, countries they have been to etc. Avoid topics such as personal age, weight, salary and other subjects that many adults prefer not to make public.

In order to have permission to move during the game, students must create a sentence using a comparative. For example, Jenan and Halima establish that Jenan lives five miles away from the class, and Halima lives ten miles away. In order for Halima to move, she must say, 'I live further away than Jenan' or 'Jenan lives nearer/closer to college than I do.' Now Halima and Jenan can swap places. The students standing in line can talk to the person next to them and move themselves one person at a time into the correct final order.

This can be done in small groups with the groups racing each other to finish first. To check the order, the first student in the line says 'I live three miles from college,' the second says 'I live five miles from college' and so on. The class can applaud the group on completion.

## Connect Four

| Category | Step 2 speaking drill |
|---|---|
| Level | Beginner to intermediate |
| Group size | Split into pairs or small teams |
| Materials | Blank charts provided in the downloadable Appendix |
| Preparation | Decide on the themes or questions |

Connect Four is a well-known game where players have to make a line of four counters to win. Put players in pairs and give each one a blank copy of the chart below (Connect-Four.pdf in the Appendix) or draw a 6 down x 7 across grid on the board while students copy it down. Players decide

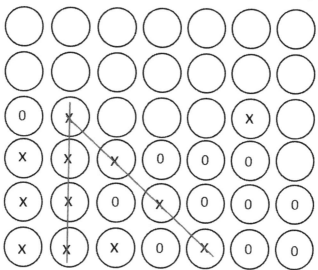

who is X and who is 0 and who is to play first, and the teacher asks the first question. This question may be anything: a vocabulary flashcard question such as 'What's this?' or a grammar question such as converting a sentence into a question or into a different tense. What you choose depends on the level of your class and what you want to drill.

If the first player can answer the question, he or she tells the opponent the answer and places an X wherever he or she likes on the bottom line. (The grid must be filled up from the bottom.) Now it's the next player's turn. He or she places an 0. Each X or 0 must either rest on the bottom row or on top of another X or 0. Each line of four made horizontally, vertically or diagonally earns a point and the game continues.

Students enjoy the challenge of trying to make four in a row while working on their English.

**Multi-level classes**     The best students might be helpers who are on call to mediate if a pair of players has a doubt about the accuracy of an answer. It can be stimulating for the better students to be given responsibility and a higher challenge than the game itself.

## Counting and Number Games for Beginners

| | |
|---|---|
| Category | Numbers – see each game for more information |
| Level | Beginners |
| Group size | Any |
| Materials | See each separate game |
| Preparation | Minimal |

### Currencies and Numbers: Guess the Price – Step 2 Speaking Drill

Hold up an item for the group to see. Each player writes down a price and the winner is the one who either guesses the price of the item or gets closest to it. To determine who wins, begin by asking any player for his or her price. You respond by saying whether the actual price is higher or lower. If it is higher, all those with lower prices know they have lost. Continue asking players for their prices until the winner is identified.

For beginners, the prices can be very simple, such as £1/$1, £3/$3 and so on. To work with more complicated numbers, price things at £1.98/$1.98¢ or £358.98p/$458.98¢. This can be done in different currencies so that learners become familiar with euros, pounds, yen, etc.

You may also divide your class into groups to play this game and elect your more able class members as group leaders, who will hold up the cards and ask for prices. Use any items such as day-to-day household objects, a dress in *Vogue*, a Ferrari, a house, food and drink items or pieces of furniture.

### Counting: Match Stick Game – Step 2 Speaking

This is the classic game where a small group of people each have three matches or similar items behind their backs. Sitting round in a circle, players take between none and three matches and hides them in their fists. All players hold out one fist in the middle of the circle, the object being to guess the total number of matches in all the hands. Each player takes a guess. If someone says six, no one else can say six in that round. Aside from numbers, this game can also be used with 'I think there are ...' 'There are ...' and 'I believe there are ...'

### Counting: Pass the Ball – Step 2 Speaking Drill

To learn to count from say 0 to 20 students pass a ball round a circle with everyone counting in unison. When the players become good at counting, have only the player passing the ball say the number. With more than 15 students, pass 2 or more balls round at once to make things more interesting.

You don't always have to start from 0. You could:

- count in tens: 10 20 30 40 50 etc.
- or count up in 2s: 2 4 6 8 10 12 etc.
- or count up in 3s: 3 6 9 12 15 etc.
- or count all numbers with a 9 in them: 9 19 29 39 49 59 69 79 89 91 92 93 etc.

When the class becomes good at this, whistle or clap to signal a change in direction so students count down instead, or instead of passing the ball around throw it to another student.

### Counting: Lottery – Step 1 Listening Drill

Ask each student to write out a five-digit number on a piece of paper. Divide the class into two teams. Call out a five-digit number for team 1. The pupils listen and if they are holding a number that contains all the digits you named they must hold it up; if correct, they win a point. (The numbers do not have to be in the same order as those that you call out.) Then call out a different five-digit number for team 2. The first team to gain two points wins the lottery. You could give the losing team a fun group forfeit. In order to be able to find winners quickly, restrict the range of numbers, say from

1 to 30. If students already know 1 to 30 well, play with a range such as 389 to 425.

## Creative Storytelling

| Category | Step 5 speaking fluency |
|---|---|
| Level | Intermediate to advanced |
| Group size | Any class size divided into groups |
| Materials | None |
| Preparation | Decide which well-known story titles you will use |

Write three or four well-known story titles – Little Red Riding Hood, or a film title such as *Four Weddings and a Funeral* – on the board. Short stories that are not too complicated work best. Make sure that whatever story you use is known by your students; if in doubt, ask them to give you the titles. Next, ask a student to recount the gist of one of the stories as briefly as possible. Ask a different student to do the same with the next story, and so on.

Now divide the class into small groups of two to four students per group and give them ten minutes to come up with a new version of the story. Keeping the characters and basic elements, students recreate a different type of story altogether: for example *Four Weddings and a Funeral* becomes a police thriller, Goldilocks becomes a horror story, Little Red Riding Hood becomes a love story and The Emperor's New Clothes becomes an adventure story. Students can add new characters, change the ending and have some creative leeway. At the end, students listen to each other's stories and judge them for entertainment value, creativity and fluency of delivery.

## Creative Writing

| Category | Step 6 creative writing |
|---|---|
| Level | Beginner to advanced |
| Group size | Any |
| Materials | None |
| Preparation | Decide which words are to be included in the story |

Students make up sentences or paragraphs using any language they like as long as certain words you specify are included. For beginners, provide simple vocabulary words such as doctor, house, dog, son, and daughter.

A beginner might come up with the following: 'I am a doctor. I live in a house. I love my dog. I have a son and a daughter.'

*With complete beginners, it is recommended to stick to families of related words. Make these as simple as you need.*

Here is another example relating to directions and places: supermarket, left, cinema, right, bank, straight on. A student might write:

'Where is the supermarket please?'

'It is on the left.'

'Thank you.'

'Where is the cinema?'

'Take the first street on the right after the bank.'

For more advanced students, the possibilities are endless. Students can describe something, make up a story, or detail how something works, etc. Adapt this idea to any area of vocabulary and specify if the story is to be in the past, present or future.

The key thing is that students are interested and motivated to express themselves, so it's best if they pick their topics. A fun way to encourage creativity is to have students pick topics for each other, which could be a kind of joke in some cases, depending on how mischievous they are. Here's an idea: give students a narrative writing challenge where each person thinks up the most boring topic possible. These are collected, shuffled and handed out again randomly. The challenge is to write a paragraph or two on the topic and try to make it sound really interesting. This is an opportunity to think, to be imaginative and for other students to learn something, as something that is dull for one might be another's passion. Students read out their creations in small groups and the group picks the best one to read to the class. (It could prove dull to listen to every single story, hence the selection process in groups!)

## Creative Writing Diary Project

| Category | Step 6 creative writing |
|---|---|
| Level | Beginner to advanced |
| Group size | Any |
| Materials | None |
| Preparation | None |

This activity can be an ongoing project over a term or several weeks. It is useful for practising the simple past with beginners, but need not be confined to that. Students keep a diary. This can be very basic for beginners, requiring only three sentences per day, such as 'Today I brushed my teeth. I ate eggs for breakfast. I walked to class.' For higher levels, you may tell students to pretend to be a character from history, or from the media – anybody they like, aside from themselves. Students can pick different characters to allow comparison, or can all be the same one.

After a week or two, students swap their diaries over and read them out. Students then try to guess the author of the diary. The student reading should continue until someone figures out who the author is. The students listening only have one guess each, so you do not have a situation where one student just calls out everyone's names.

## Creative Writing With Adjectives

| Category | Step 6 creative writing or Step 2 speaking drill |
| --- | --- |
| Level | Beginner to advanced |
| Group size | Any |
| Materials | Pictures of people or scenes |
| Preparation | None |

For this activity you'll need a number of images of people or scenes. These could be of simple things for beginners, such as a tall person or a large lady, to controversial scenes from history or photos you find in the papers. For every picture you show, beginner students need to come up with at least one adjective; advanced students could think up five per picture.

Students then write a sentence containing adjectives of their choice. In a mixed-ability class, you may want to have beginners and lower intermediates working in pairs so they can help each other if lacking in vocabulary.

You may also use this activity as a speaking exercise. Show the picture, let people call out adjectives and let others make up sentences. With a large group, hand out at least one picture to every three students. Students hold up a picture and say the adjective they have thought of, then pass the picture to a colleague who suggests a different adjective (complete beginners may need to repeat the same adjective for lack of vocabulary). As an option, put students in teams and award points for correct or colourful adjectives.

## Cryptic Clues

| | |
|---|---|
| Category | Step 2 speaking drill with creative writing option |
| Group size | Any |
| Level | Lower intermediate to advanced |
| Materials | Written clues and optional use of pictures |
| Preparation | Use the clues found in the downloadable Appendix, or the riddles, have students prepare some for homework |

Spread your clues out around the room (adapt them to the language ability of your group). For example, if the item is a television, clues could be, 'You sit in front of this at home,' 'You watch it' or 'This is known for its entertainment value.' If the item is a watch, clues could be, 'What time is it?' or 'It tells the time.' For higher abilities, clues could be made more cryptic, for example 'You can watch it pass but you cannot stop it' (time!).

Players mill about looking for the clues and work out the items as they go. Allow a time limit for this project. Then let the class compare answers with each other. There is no need for you to mark this work or check answers. The class can ask you if there are clues unsolved at the end.

To help your students and to make things easier, play as above, but also stick up pictures of the items around the room. Allow a few minutes during which time players read the clues and find the matching items.

**Creative Writing Option**     The class works in small groups to come up with a series of clues for another team to guess. This task could be a homework assignment. Have a play off – see who has the best clues and who can answer them.

## Debates

| | |
|---|---|
| Category | Step 5 speaking fluency |
| Level | Intermediate to advanced |
| Group size | Any – students work in pairs |
| Materials | None |
| Preparation | Decide on the topics to be discussed |

There are many ways to carry out a debate in class. Here are some ideas.

Firstly, choose your subject with care. I recommend checking with the class before launching a topic to make sure that there is no one present who strongly objects to a particular discussion: there may be someone undergoing deep personal grief over an issue (such as not being able to get pregnant) and your discussion on abortion or IVF may cause unnecessary distress. Generally, steer clear of 'red-hot' issues such as abortion, religion and current political situations. These topics usually arouse hostility and it is likely that a few students who feel strongly about the issue will take over rather than letting everyone have a chance to speak. Often, a heavy topic leads to a heavy atmosphere, and your lesson might not be the place for that.

It's often best to ask students what they would like to debate. This is also a good idea because the discussion may be more likely to interest them than a topic you choose. Teenagers may be utterly bored by the idea of discussing environmental energy sources, while you find the topic absorbing!

1. Put students in pairs and write a statement on the board for them to debate. One student takes one side of the argument while the other argues against him or her. One side must argue for the topic regardless of personal opinions while the other side must argue against. This prevents discussions becoming too heated and allows for a student to role-play rather than express personal views. Rotate the students to give them the opportunity to present their arguments again to a fresh person – they should notice that they become more and more fluent!

2. Put the topic up on the board and tell students to get into small groups and discuss it briefly between themselves with a view to making up their minds – rapidly – as to which side of the argument they will take. Next, send all those who agree with the statement to one side of the room and all those who do not to the other. Ask the students to get together again in small groups and quickly come up with as many points to argue their view with as they can. While they are doing this, count up how many students are for and against the debate motion, and note this on the board.

3. Explain that there will be a debate and that the aim is to win people over to your side. Then put the students in pairs or very small groups made up of a mix of students from each side of the argument and allow them to discuss the issue together. Then take a vote. Count up the votes for and

against the argument at the end to see what the overall is, and whether many people, if any, changed sides as a result of the discussion.

4. Divide students into an even number of groups, such as eight groups of students made of up two or three people per group. Give each pair of groups one topic to discuss. One group is for, and one against. These can be light hearted or serious. Preferably, ask students for topics they find interesting and use those. One group, for example, has the topic that cities are bad places to live and must agree with the statement while the other group has the same topic and must disagree with it. Allow five minutes for the groups to discuss their topics and to work out their arguments. Now put the two groups together. One argues for their topic, but the group opposite must disagree with whatever is said, regardless of what students really think, and say why.

Teacher Chris Yates (who has this book) wrote to me about his fun and informative way of debating, which re-enacts how political debates are carried out in the UK. *'We do them in the style of the House of Commons,'* he wrote. *'Having gone through the mechanics, rehearsed it a few times, we watch a quick YouTube video of a parliamentary session (which they find hilarious) – then I appoint a pupil to be Mr or Mrs Speaker and give him or her a gavel. The others have to say "hear, hear" after each speech or rebuttal (until the Speaker calls them to order!). I generally make the timid or weaker students the Speaker, as it puts them in a position of power or authority.*

*'Like you suggest, I stick to non-contentious subjects: "This House believes cats are better than dogs," or "This House prefers motorbikes to cars." I find the more silly the argument, the more they play up the theatricality, and can also concentrate on getting the English right. If pupils actually believe in the substance of the debate, they get tied up in knots trying to make genuine and complex points, and the whole thing becomes a bit fraught.*

*'Rebuttals are good for practising reported speech ("Mr Speaker: we have heard my honourable friend say that cats are cleaner than dogs. That may be so. But, Mr Speaker, what good is a cat when a burglar breaks into your house?")*

*'I then get them to argue the opposite case, so the pro-cats are now the anti-cats, etc. I think this bit is actually the most important.*

*'Behind all this, the activity shows what democracy is or how democratic arguments should be conducted – with respect for those who differ in opinion, and cultural backgrounds to parliamentary systems.'*

Thanks, Chris, for your excellent ideas.

Here are some potential topics for debate.

- Is a dishonest act ever ethical?
- Should we store our dead in cemeteries?
- The amount of money you earn is in direct proportion to the number of people you reach with your product or service. Discuss.
- Life was better 20 years ago than it is now.
- How far should we go to keep people alive? (Take care!)
- How far should we go to help people have children? (I would avoid this topic myself.)
- There's no harm in plastic surgery.
- The church plays a key role in society today. (I would avoid this ...)
- Humans will destroy the earth.
- Politics is the most important profession there is.
- Public transport is better than everyone owning private vehicles.
- Living in the city is better than living in the country.
- Marriage is an outdated institution and serves no purpose. (Take care.)
- It's not natural to spend your whole life with one partner. (Again, handle with care.)
- It's ethical to eat animals. (Ditto.)
- Latin should be taught in schools and be available to all children as a choice. (Replace Latin with a more relevant language/subject if necessary.)
- Young children should concentrate on the arts rather than learning to read and write.
- There's no point to travel – after all, we can watch documentaries on TV.

For teenagers:

- Parents know more about life than teenagers and teenagers should listen to them.
- Teenagers should not have to go to school but should be allowed to start work at 14.
- Should your parents give you money or should you have to earn it? Why? How much is reasonable? And what is it for?

### Magic wand idea for future tense, conditionals and modals

*You have just found a magic wand that allows you to change three things in your life, such as your job, your school, your town, or whatever you decide. You are allowed to change anything you want. How would you change yourself, your school, your job ...? Have students discuss why they feel these changes are important. Another variation is to have them discuss what they would change if they become a headteacher, boss or prime minister for a month.*

## Decision Time

| Category | Step 5 speaking fluency – what would you do? |
|---|---|
| Level | Intermediate |
| Group size | Any |
| Materials | None |
| Preparation | Decide on topics students will decide on |

Give students a scenario and ask them what they would do. Ideas are crimes and punishments, social security and taxation, illegal immigrants, someone entering a church in shorts, etc. Choose topics that are suitable for your culture that will not offend but that are sufficiently interesting (see the debates section above for ideas). After doing this once, ask students to prepare 'What would you do?' scenarios for homework and use these in class.

Students circulate asking the others what they would do and grouping themselves together with those who think the same way. At the end you will have several groups of like-minded students. The aim for students is to collect as many people as possible together in their group. The biggest group wins.

## Describe The Picture

| Category | Step 5 speaking fluency – there is, there are, prepositions, present continuous |
|---|---|
| Level | Beginner to lower intermediate |
| Group size | Any |
| Materials | Pictures |

| Preparation | Find three suitable pictures – a demonstration picture is provided in the Appendix |
|---|---|

Students work in pairs or small groups. One student describes a picture without showing it to the others, who listen and try to draw the picture. Pictures with family groups in the home are useful for beginners learning about family members, rooms of the house and household objects. You are likely to find suitable pictures in your textbook, if you use one. Postcards and magazines may also provide good images. Students may also be given the task of finding a good picture to describe for homework, but you will need spares for those who were absent, who forgot, or who did not have time to do it.

You need one picture to use for the demonstration and then two different pictures for the pair work. Either distribute the same two pictures to all students or allow students to use the pictures they have brought in. If setting the picture-finding task for homework, do a demonstration with the students first, with you describing the picture and the students drawing. Students will therefore know exactly why the picture is required and can choose something that they are able to describe.

Pre-taught phrases such as 'in the foreground', 'in the background', 'to the side' will be useful.

Drawing the picture is not a requirement – the student listening can simply imagine the picture being described, and then afterwards compare the real picture with the one he or she imagined.

**Describe The Word**

| Category | Step 5 speaking fluency |
|---|---|
| Level | Intermediate to advanced |
| Group size | Any |
| Materials | None |
| Preparation | Prepare a list of things for students to describe |

Introduce to students the purpose of the game, which is to describe words. This is useful, as sometimes one can be at a loss for a vocabulary word and have to describe what one is trying to say. In addition, this activity allows students to use a wide range of language, which helps speaking fluency.

Divide students into small teams or pairs. They think up objects that they know how to describe and race to describe as many objects as possible to their pair or team members within a given timeframe. Alternatively, you may find it beneficial to provide students with a list of words they should describe, and this is useful for reviewing specific vocabulary. To be on the safe side, have lists of words ready to use if your students cannot think up words on their own.

If students cannot guess a word, players can move on to avoid getting stuck. With lower intermediates, you may allow the simplest of descriptions, such as 'You write with it' to describe a pen. With more advanced students, give the team only one guess. This means that the person describing the object has to be as detailed as possible to have the best chance of gaining the team point. For example: 'It is a large animal with big ears and a trunk and it is usually grey.' 'It is a small, flat, rectangular piece of plastic that you use to pay for things.' Another way of making the game suitable for advanced students is to give them a list of words to describe that are not basic nouns but concepts or emotions, such as timid, feeling blue, insurance, assurance, vitality. Do this as pair work or in small teams.

Once students know this game, you may set them the task of preparing words and descriptions for homework for use in the next class. Students should be motivated to prepare difficult words for opposite teams to guess.

With a multi-level class, let the higher levels describe the words while the lower levels try to guess what they are.

## Detective Game

| | |
|---|---|
| Category | Step 2 speaking drill |
| Group size | Small group to a class of up to about 30 |
| Level | Beginner to intermediate |
| Materials | None |
| Preparation | None |

**How to play**    One student is chosen to be the detective and one the thief. The detective has three chances to find the thief, which he or she does by asking a question to three students of his or her choosing. The question can take any question form you like, such as 'What is your name?' 'Where do you live?' 'What were you doing last night?' etc. The three students answer the questions accordingly, and if one of them is the thief he or she must give himself up for arrest after answering the questions. If the detective has not found the thief after asking three questions, he or she got away, so now choose a new thief and a new detective for the next round.

The above set-up works well for a small group of students. If you have a larger group, then pick more thieves and detectives to ask and answer questions simultaneously so that more people are involved in speaking.

A way to spice the game up is to allow the detective to ask as many students as many questions as possible in a given timeframe. If you have some kind of timer that ticks audibly, this adds an element of excitement. Allow the detective one minute only to find the thief and then play another round with a different detective. If you divide the whole class into two teams, you can record which team finds the most thieves during the course of the game.

### *Variation*

Another way in which to use this same idea but within a different scenario is to reverse the procedure. Instead of the detective trying to find the thief, you could have a situation where the student asking the question does not want to find the culprit. For example, you could have a thief who robs your house if you speak to him or her. The questioner asks three students a question. If one of those three is the thief, the detective has his or her house robbed, so that team can lose a point.

## Dictation

| | |
|---|---|
| Category | Step 1 listening drill |
| Group size | Any |
| Level | Beginner to intermediate |
| Materials | None |
| Preparation | Decide on the text you will dictate |

Although this is a pretty unimaginative way to teach, once in a while it can be utilized as a listening and writing exercise. If used occasionally, it can be fun.

If you do decide to give dictation a go, do not dictate slowly, word for word, but read out whole sentences at normal speaking speeds and repeat several times. This is much more challenging than writing down detached individual words and makes for a more meaningful experience for students, who have to listen more intently and also hear language being used in context.

Dictation is useful as a listening activity when introducing new grammar. After using the rapid-dictation method just described, write the correct sentences on the board, and let students check their work quickly at the end.

## Directions

| | |
|---|---|
| Category | Step 2 speaking drill |
| Group size | Any |
| Level | Beginner to intermediate |
| Materials | None |
| Preparation | None |

Draw a grid on the board and write some numbers or letters in each square. Blindfold a student and tell him or her to circle a particular number or letter by following the directions given by the rest of the class. To add some fun, divide the class and the board into two or three sections, and let each team guide a team member and try to beat the other teams to accomplish the task.

### *Variation*

A variant for small groups is for 'seeing' students to guide blindfolded students through the classroom from one end to the other, without touching any furniture.

GAMES E–G

## Either/Or

| Category | Step 5 speaking fluency |
|---|---|
| Level | Intermediate to advanced |
| Group size | Any – put large classes in teams |
| Materials | None |
| Preparation | Decide on some either/or things your students will use |

A student comes up with an either/or phrase such as 'love or hate'. The next student proposes another choice, such as 'earth or sky'. For a fun way to play, use the Relay Race idea to pass these choices along a team. With intermediate students, the same phrase can be passed all the way down the line for reinforcement. Each team member must come up with one phrase, which is passed up or down the line. Advanced students can play by each coming up with something original.

Here is a selection of examples to show you how vast the possibilities are for language: trick or treat, big or small, valley or mountain, fat or thin, tea or coffee, near or far, bigger or smaller, little or large, carnivore or vegetarian, business or pleasure, more or less, here or there, now or later, true or false, etc.

Take any either/or idea and let students pass a message down the line, arguing which is better: trick or treat, big or small, valley or mountain and so on. Students argue for either big or little and define the context of their argument. For example, 'Little is better because if you eat a big plate of food you get fat.' 'And little is also better because little feet are prettier than big feet.' 'Little is better because little rooms cost less to heat' and so on. Or 'Big is better because there is more room in a big car.' 'Big is better because if you are hungry a big plate of food is better than a small one.' 'Near is better because it takes no time to get there.' 'Far is better because it is exciting and exotic …'

If this is too difficult and students cannot think of anything quickly enough, instead, write the 'either' words on the board and let students think of 'ors' that could go with them, preferably in teams to give an edge to the activity.

## English Trivia

| Category | Step 2 speaking drill – revision |
|---|---|
| Level | All levels |
| Group size | Any – put large classes into small groups |
| Materials | See the Appendix for ready-made boards and card sets, and blanks to make your own categories. One board game per group |
| Preparation | None once you have the board and questions – see Appendix |

This game works like Trivial Pursuit, but instead of general knowledge questions you need questions involving English, such as vocabulary, tenses, forming questions and general grammar. Make a category for any grammatical topic you like. For an easier game, use limited topics such as vocabulary words for sports, the present tense and other language areas you have studied recently. For a broader revision game, widen the topics to include all vocabulary, all tenses and so on.

Students can make their own boards on a piece of A4 paper by copying down the design you draw on the board. Eventually, you might make some fancy boards using card, but a simple pattern of squares with a start and a finish are sufficient. Some squares will be blue, some red, some green and some yellow. These colours correspond to a language category. Students roll a die and when they land on a coloured square they take a card from the relevant category and answer the question.

For beginners, these could be picture cards, which they must name. For grammar, picture cards of actions work well, and students must, for example, put the action into a sentence, using the present continuous. For intermediates, you might have a sentence written out in the present tense, and the task is to put it into the past tense.

Students call on the teacher to verify an answer if no one in the group is sure.

## Figure It Out

| Category | Step 6 creative writing |
|---|---|
| Group size | Any |

| Level | Beginner to advanced |
|---|---|
| Materials | Pictures or words – see the Appendix for ready-made example sets |
| Preparation | None – use the example sets in the Appendix for a demo and then have students prepare more for homework to use in a future class |

Prepare sets of picture cards or words to each represent a theme. For example, a beach would include sand, water, sunglasses and sun tan oil. Place these sets around the room if students can get up and move around. Failing that, use the board. Allow a time limit for the task and let everyone decipher the clues – the pictures – to find the word that connects them. You may require students to make up a sentence containing the word, or that they write a paragraph, or a story using all the words. For beginners, identifying the word may be enough.

Let students work in pairs to encourage interaction in English between them.

### Variation

To add a little fun, prepare one set of clues per person, or pair of people. Hand these out face down. On the word 'Go!' students turn over their cards and have 20 seconds to decipher the clues. You then call out 'Pass!' All students pass their cards to the person/pair behind them and take a new set from the person in front. Allow only a few seconds for the swap. At the end, go through the answers.

Here are examples:
- chocolate cake: chocolate, flour, butter and cake decoration
- police station: policemen, handcuffs, building and parking ticket
- hairdresser: hairbrush, scissors, money and mirror
- car: wheels, steering wheel, map or GPS and baby seat
- fashion show: stilettoes, lipstick, hairdryer and clothes
- cinema: ticket, 3D glasses, popcorn and ice cream
- television: sofa, remote control and a potato (for couch potato – someone who watches TV often)
- snowman: cold, white, man and carrot

Make some clues easy and others more cryptic for a challenge. Students can prepare further sets of clues for homework.

## Fill In Drill

| Category | Step 2 speaking drill |
|---|---|
| Group size | Any |
| Level | Beginner to intermediate |
| Materials | None |
| Preparation | Choose a written passage or dialogue from your textbook or write one |

On the board, prepare a letter, short story or dialogue using grammar and vocabulary you have been teaching recently or would like to review. Let the class read it out and check everyone understands by asking a couple of questions about the text. Next, tell students to read the first sentence carefully. Now erase one word from that sentence and have a class member read it out again and fill in the blank (from memory) with the missing word you just removed. Now remove a second word from the sentence and ask another student to read it out again. This should be very easy and serves for a clear demonstration. Now divide the class into pairs and have them take it in turns to read out the sentences on the board. As time goes on, you gradually rub out more and more words. As an alternative to pair work, play this game with the whole class, reading out the letter and filling in the blanks together in unison.

Here is an example of text using conditionals.

'What would you do if you won the lottery?'

'I would first donate ten per cent to charity and then I would give some to my family. I expect my brother would buy a new car right away. He'd get a Ferrari knowing him. Of course, that would depend on how much money I gave him, which would depend on how much I had won in the first place.'

Start by deleting words such as 'would' and 'won' rather than 'lottery', or delete verbs and little words rather than nouns first. Start slowly and listen in to see how students are doing. Delete more words when you see that they are coping. Too few words being deleted will mean that the task is too easy; too many will make it too hard, so err on the side of caution. Too easy is better than too hard, because at least students are drilling accurate English. To help students, delete part of a word and leave the first letter as a clue.

# Find The Pairs Memory Game – Vocabulary, Grammar

| Category | Step 2 speaking drill |
|---|---|
| Group size | Small groups |
| Level | Beginner to intermediate |
| Materials | Two sets of matching picture or word cards. You need matching sets of pictures without words for learning vocabulary, where pictures are better than words. For grammar, use word cards, and have students make sentences with them |
| Preparation | Try the example set in the Appendix, or fill in the blank set for your purposes |

**How to play**    This game is also known as Concentration. Take two sets of identical pictures, shuffle them and spread them out face down. The pictures can be laid out randomly or in a grid. Player 1 turns over two cards and names the items. If they are a pair, player 1 keeps the cards. If they are not a pair, he or she turns them back over, leaving them face down in the same place. Player 2 now turns over two cards, attempting to turn over two identical pictures, while naming the items. The game continues until all the pairs have been found.

In the classic game, when a player turns over a pair he or she gets another go. However, as the goal is to have the group talking rather than find a winner, I prefer to let each person have only one turn. This makes it less likely for the more able person to win all the pairs, leaving the others with nothing.

A nice way to keep everyone interested even when it is not their turn, aside from the fact that they are supposed to be remembering where the cards are, is to split your group into two teams. Each person has a turn as normal; however, if he or she cannot name an item, then the team members can help. If a pair is turned over but the team cannot name the vocabulary, they forfeit winning that pair. When counting up all the pairs at the end, you can have a winning team rather than a winning individual.

**Language ideas**    The language possibilities to use with this game are unlimited. Keep an eye – as always – on the complexity, so that the game does not drag.

Vocabulary – each player simply names the item on the cards as he or she turns them over.

Phrases – each player forms a short phrase including the item on the card. For example, with pictures of people, one could use adjectives such as 'a pretty girl', 'a tall boy', or with places 'a big city' or 'a small village'.

Sentences – each player forms a sentence using one or both of the items. For example, if you are using pictures of food, players could say 'I like butter and milk,' or 'I like butter but I don't like milk.' If you are using pictures of people, players could say 'Her name is Claudia,' 'She is a dentist,' 'She is from Spain' or 'She is wearing trousers.' You can also work on comparatives – 'The girl is taller than the boy' or 'The girl is older than the baby.' More advanced students can use more complicated structures, depending on the language you would like them to use. For example, 'I was going to buy some milk but I bought some cheese instead,' or 'I have never been to London but I have been to Paris.'

Questions – players can ask questions related to each picture they turn over. For example, with sets of people, one could ask 'What's her name?' or 'Where does she live?' or 'How old is she?' With two teams, one can also have one team ask the players in the other team a question that they answer on turning over two cards. For example, Team 1 asks 'Where did you go last summer?' and the player from Team 2 who turns over the two cards replies 'I went to London and Paris.'

### Find The Pairs Memory Game – Pronunciation, Spelling

| | |
|---|---|
| Category | Step 3 spelling drill and pronunciation |
| Group size | Small groups |
| Level | Intermediate to advanced |
| Materials | Two sets of matching word cards |
| Preparation | Fill in the blank set from the appendix with words of your choosing (Find-The-Pairs.pdf) |

Play as above, but use words that rhyme. Easy words suit beginners, such as cat and pat, whereas for advanced students, words with silent letters or homophone pairs – words that sounds exactly the same but with different spellings, such as nose and knows – may be used.

Here are examples of rhyming words that have different spelling:
- light, might, kite, site, sight, slight
- bridge, fridge, carriage, marriage
- few, dew, do, to, threw, you, through

- sew, mow, sow, go, though, dough
- buy, cry, die, fly, sigh, my, tie, lie
- leek, tweak, peak, peek
- eat, sheet, meet, meat
- some, dumb, thumb, mum, plum
- cake, bake, break, shake, make
- we, see, tea, me, fee
- hair, flare, snare, glare, air, pear, fair, fare, tear (to rip)
- saw, bore, gnaw, floor, tore
- learn, turn, fern
- sent, cent, per cent
- whether, weather, together, forever
- rose, rows, goes, shows
- loud, rowed, cloud, allowed
- wood, would, could, good, should
- there, their, they're

## Fizz Buzz

| | |
|---|---|
| Category | Step 2 speaking drill |
| Group size | Small groups of up to 12 |
| Level | Beginner to intermediate |
| Materials | None |
| Preparation | None |

Have all your players sit round in a circle of 12 people maximum. The first player says '1', the next says '2', and the next says '3', and so on. Now add in a new element – every time the number 2 comes up, or a number with 2 in it (such as 12, 20, 22, 26, etc.), the player must say 'fizz' instead of the number. For example, 1 fizz 3 4 5 6 7 8 9 10 11 fizz 13 14 15 16 17 18 19 fizz fizz fizz etc. up to 30, then 31, fizz, 33 etc.

Once the group has mastered this idea to some degree, throw in another element, such as any number with a 5 in it becomes 'buzz'. This would give 1 fizz 3 4 buzz 6 7 8 9 10 11 fizz 13 14 buzz 16 etc.

To make things really complicated, say that any number that can be divided by 2 or 5 is a fizz buzz.

**Language ideas**       This fun game can also be used to revise vocabulary. Here is an example. Using animal vocabulary, have a rule where any animal ending in an r is followed by fizz, and any animal ending in a t is followed by buzz, any animal ending in an e is followed by fizz buzz. A round might look like this: tiger, fizz, antelope, fizz buzz, elephant, buzz, ant, buzz, lion, duck, bird, crocodile, fizz buzz, etc.

This game is quite tricky and you would definitely want to precede it with something like Brainstorm to refresh everyone's memory of animal vocabulary.

## Forfeits

Ask the students to come up with their own ideas of forfeits they find acceptable for homework. Below is a list of mostly sensible ideas for forfeits that can be used in many games.

- name-a-picture flashcard
- spell out a word
- make a sentence or a question using the target language
- ask a friend any question in English
- name three things you like
- answer – in a full sentence – a question such as 'Do you have a sister?'
- balance a ball on your head for three seconds
- bounce a ball saying 10, 20, 30 etc. up to 100
- spell your name backwards
- count to 10 from any number such as 51 to 63
- yawn until you make someone else yawn
- do a sum such as 70 minus 60
- say a tongue twister (see Tongue Twisters for ideas)
- stand on one leg and do not smile for 10 seconds
- try and make someone else laugh in 10 seconds
- look at someone and do not smile for a full minute
- say a sentence about kangaroos, or elephants, or any topic
- intermediates say two or three sentences about a topic
- advanced students give a spontaneous one-minute talk
- the topic can be serious or silly, such as 'Why I want a pet cobra'

## Gap Fill Game

| Category | Step 3 writing drill |
| --- | --- |
| Group size | All class sizes |

73

| Level | Beginner to intermediate |
|---|---|
| Materials | Prepared sentences with matching gap fills – see the Appendix for an example |
| Preparation | Prepare your gap fills, take them from your textbook, or make them |

Here is an easy and fun writing game. You need some room between desks, as this game involves some walking around the class. It is to be played once your students are familiar with necessary vocabulary and sentences and is particularly good for drilling specific grammar.

**How to play**    Divide the class into pairs. Each student has a sheet with sentences that you want to work on. With a big class, give each student three sentences, and with a smaller group use more. These sheets with the full sentences stay on the students' desks. Spread out gap fills around the room that match the full sentences students have on their desks.

Students need remember the first sentence on their sheet that stays on their desks. They then move around searching for the corresponding gap fill while keeping the full sentence in their mind. This ensures that mental effort is made to remember.

Once a student has found the corresponding gap fill exercise, he or she fills it in and returns to his or her desk to memorize the second sentence, and then finds and completes the gap fill version of this sentence. Put students in teams and see which team finishes first.

**Language ideas**    Use any sentence or question form in any tense. For beginners, stick to short sentences and use only known vocabulary when dealing with a new grammar point. Use only one grammatical form when presenting new grammar, but mix up all sorts of sentences for a revision exercise. See the Appendix for an example using negatives.

**Get Moving**

| Category | Step 5 speaking fluency |
|---|---|
| Group size | Up to 24 in 2 groups |
| Level | High beginner to advanced |
| Materials | None |
| Preparation | None |

This game relaxes students and allows them to be creative. Use it if you feel students are becoming lethargic. Get them standing up and refresh their energy so they can concentrate better on what follows.

This game is mostly useful for vocabulary revision. It's on upstagereview.org as The Martha Game, with an unknown author.

Make a space in the classroom. A student moves into the space and forms an object with his or her body saying, for example, 'I'm a tree.' The next student runs in to the space and becomes something else: 'I'm a leaf on the tree.' The next student becomes a bench under the tree, and the next a bottom on the bench, the next a dog weeing on the tree and the next a newspaper being read.

This game must be speedy to be fun. Any student who is ready can run into the space and join the 'picture'. If you have two groups, let them alternate, and repeat the exercise so that students get better at thinking on their feet. They may be shy at first, but will loosen up.

In future lessons, once every student in the group has joined the picture, make it a talking picture.

## Getting To Know You

| Category | Step 5 speaking fluency |
|---|---|
| Level | Beginner to intermediate |
| Group size | Any – put large classes in teams |
| Materials | None |
| Preparation | None |

This is a good way for students to get to know each other and develop fluency. Divide the students into two teams. A student from team A makes a statement about someone on team B, such as 'Salim, you like tea.' Salim answers with true or false. If Salim answers 'true', team A wins a point. Now it is a student from team B's turn to make a statement about a member of team A, such as 'Marta, you play tennis.' Marta answers with true or false, and so on. Tell the students that they must be honest, or the game is no fun. You may like to award points for correctly formed statements. This motivates students to take more care. However, you may like to play a faster pace and let some errors go. You can always write corrections on the board to review later. Ask for a similar statement using the same construction so students have a chance to hear it said properly.

With a small group, use a free-for-all approach, where any student can contribute as soon as he or she has thought of a statement.

Alternatively, let the students take turns in a more structured way. With a large group you may need four teams and have two separate games going on simultaneously.

## Good Evening Beach Ball

| | |
|---|---|
| Category | Step 2 speaking drill, easy warm-up |
| Group size | Best with smaller groups |
| Level | Beginner to lower intermediate |
| Materials | A beach ball you have written on |
| Preparation | None |

Buy a beach ball or any cheap softball that can be written on. Using a marker pen, divide up the ball into segments, and write a friendly greeting in each segment such as 'Good evening [teacher's name]!' or 'How do you do?' or 'How are you?' If you use a pen that washes off, you will be able to use the same beach ball for different sentences. It's probably easier to have a couple of different balls written on in permanent pen, as you may want to reuse them with your different classes.

This activity works particularly well with sleepy students in an evening class. It wakes up tired businesspeople and takes the pressure off for a while – when they catch the ball, all they have to do is read out the phrase that their thumbs are pointing to, then throw the ball to the next person. You'll understand what an impact this class opener can have when you walk in one day and a student who never says anything without being prompted grins and greets you with 'Good evening, Shelley!'

### *Variation*

As an optional competitive element, if someone makes a grammatical error, this is the equivalent of dropping the ball, so that student loses a point for his or her team. Alternatively, the student's penalty could be to go down on one knee. If he or she answers his or her next question correctly, he or she stands back up again, but if there's another error he or she must next catch the ball one-handed, and so on, so that it becomes progressively harder to catch. Note that no one should be forced to do this, and be sensitive to any students feeling humiliated or exposed

## Grammar Auction

| | |
|---|---|
| Category | Step 3 grammar |

| Group size | Two or more |
| --- | --- |
| Level | Beginner to advanced |
| Materials | Sentences |
| Preparation | Write out the sentences on large strips of paper, or prepare the sentences ready to write on the board |

This game is based on a public auction, but students aren't buying antiques – they are bidding on sentences. The object is to buy the sentences that are grammatically correct and avoid the ones that have errors in them. This exercise has several useful purposes: to review previously taught grammar, to develop editing skills and allow for a review of currency units played with fake money.

You will need a number of sentences written out on strips that can be seen from the back of the room. If you can, use chart paper or pre-cut sentence strip paper about two feet wide with letters about three inches high, but strips made from any paper is fine. You could also just write the sentences on the board and write points and initials of the purchaser next to it during the auction.

There should be about three sentences per student and about half of them should contain errors. Vary the level of difficulty and the number of errors, but be sure to stick to grammar points that have been previously taught.

You will also need counters or fake currency for the students to bid with. Either give them an amount to keep track of (embedding mathematics) or hand out play money (currency and mathematics). Make sure that all the students have plenty of money, since the object is to keep them bidding all the way through the game.

**How to play**    The teacher stands at the front of the room with the sentences and holds them up one at a time. If the students think the sentence is correct, then they bid on it. Students can work in pairs or singly. Each student or pair of students will bid against each other for the sentences that they think have no errors.

When a student outbids everyone else for a sentence, the teacher notes on it the name of the student and the amount paid.

At the end of the auction the teacher goes through the sentences. If a sentence was correct, then the student gets the same amount of points as he or she paid for it. If a sentence has one or more errors, then the class corrects it together, and the student who bought it loses the same number of points as he or she paid for it. If a sentence is correct but no one bought it, then all the students lose 100 points. The student with the most points, or money, at the end is the winner!

*A word on troubleshooting. If you have a student who bids his or her entire amount on one sentence because he or she is so sure it is correct, then next time you play have a rule where students must buy a minimum of three sentences each or face a penalty.*

*To check that your students are not bidding more money than they actually have, at the end tally up the winner's points and check that he or she does not have more points than the original sum of money given out at the beginning. This is one reason why you write the name and amount on the sentence strip.*

## Grammar Drill

| Category | Step 2 speaking drill |
|---|---|
| Group size | Any |
| Level | Beginner to intermediate |
| Materials | Pictures or words – the cards for Subject–Verb–Object in the Appendix could be used for this |
| Preparation | None |

**How to play**   The students sit in a circle with a pile of picture cards face down in the middle. One student turns over a picture card and makes a specified sentence including that word.

Students should work in groups of up to eight in order to avoid too much delay between turns. Make sure a strong student is present in each group, if possible, as group leader. You circulate and monitor as much as possible. If you have a large class working in several groups that are difficult for you to monitor, then do some drills by way of demonstration before beginning so that the structure of the game sinks in, as it is most important that students make accurate sentences.

Use this activity as a dry drill and most adults will be happy, or turn it into a game. For example, you may use any kind of game board and let players advance five squares every time they make a sentence that is accurate. In addition, keep all players involved at all times and not just when it is their turn by asking them to listen and decide whether a sentence is correct or not. Players may also advance by a given number of squares for correctly assessing a sentence. The players should take equal turns in assessing sentences as well as in making them. If your students are not keen on individual competition, put them into two teams, and have just one piece on the board that represents all the adults on that team. This has the advantage of not showing up any student who is weaker than the others.

### *Variations*

A way to spice up the game is to use forfeits. If a student makes a mistake, he or she loses a life; when he or she has lost three lives, a forfeit is in order! See the Forfeits section for ideas.

Another way to add some fun is to use a timer set to go off every few minutes. The student making a sentence when the timer goes off has to say a tongue twister, do some kind of forfeit, or loses some points.

Basic sentence examples
- Food and 'I like ...' / 'I don't like ...'

Place a pile of food pictures face down. Students pick a card and say whether or not they like that food.
- Professions and 'I'm a ...

Students pick a card and say 'I'm a ...'
- Places and 'I'm from ...'

Students pick a city or country and say 'I'm from ...'

Basic grammar examples
- Present simple

Have two piles of pictures, one of people and one of professions. Students turn over one picture from each pile and make the corresponding sentence, such as 'He's a doctor.'
- Present continuous

Again, have two piles of pictures, one of people and one of actions. Students turn over one picture from each pile and make a sentence such as 'She is eating.'
- Past simple

Use two piles of pictures, such as people and actions. Students pick two cards and make the sentence such as 'She walked the dog.'
- Prepositions

Use two piles of pictures, such as objects and furniture. Students make sentences such as 'The ball is under the table.'

*The same ideas can be used to work with any tense or grammatical structure. If you do not have pictures, use word flashcards instead. The advantage of using pictures is that it helps revise vocabulary at the same time as drilling sentence structure or grammar.*

## Grammar Knock Out

| | |
|---|---|
| Category | Step 1 listening drill |
| Group size | Any |
| Level | All levels |
| Materials | None |
| Preparation | Prepare the sentences you will use during the game if you cannot think of them off the cuff |

Use this game in order to learn new grammar. Let the students listen to a new grammar structure such as 'Did you go to the cinema last night?' two or three times. On the board, explain the grammar in question, and show how the sentence is built. Now read out a selection of similar questions one by one and let the students say whether they are right or wrong. Students put their hands up for right and leave their hands on the desks if wrong. Start by reading out questions that are all correct; then gradually slip in some errors, such as 'Did you go to the shops tomorrow?' 'Did you went to the shops?' 'Did you bought some tomatoes yesterday?' If students put their hands up for these sentences, have other students explain the errors.

A variant with a small group is to go around in a circle with students taking it in turns to say whether your statement is right or wrong. If students get an answer wrong, they lose a life; when they lose three lives, they do a forfeit. You may review a wide range of tenses and grammatical structures for more advanced students and stick to a limited amount of basic phrases for beginners.

## Guess The Action

| | |
|---|---|
| Category | Step 2 speaking drill – good for present and past continuous |
| Group size | Any |
| Level | Beginner to lower intermediate |
| Materials | Word flashcards or a list of the actions you want mimed |

| Preparation | None |
|---|---|

**How to play**   For present continuous and/or vocabulary, divide the class into two teams. Show team A a picture of an action or a word flashcard. Team A mimes that action and team B has to guess what Team A is doing, using the present continuous.

For past continuous and/or vocabulary, divide the class into two teams. Team A faces the wall while you show team B an action, which they mime until you say 'Freeze.' Team A turns around and guesses what team B was doing.

*If you have a large class, play with four teams instead of two. Each student in the team guessing has one guess. Every correct guess earns a point for that team. A points system gives you a valid excuse to get all the students to use the target language. To keep the pace up, use simple sentences that are easy to act out. Sports and action verbs such as running or jumping and hobbies are obvious examples.*

### Guess The Meaning Of Dates And Numbers

| Category | Speaking fluency, asking questions |
|---|---|
| Group size | Any |
| Level | Lower intermediate and up |
| Materials | None |
| Preparation | Can be done on the spur of the moment |

Students guess the meaning of numbers in groups by asking questions. For example: 1982, 3, 74 are one student's year of birth, the number of children he or she has and the bus number he or she usually takes to class. Dates and could be for historical events, such as the end of a war, the election of a famous president and the year of a revolution. Numbers can be related to general knowledge, such as how many countries there are in South America, how many in Europe and how many in Africa.

### Guess the Question

| Category | Step 2 speaking drill for grammar review |
|---|---|
| Group size | Better with fewer students |

| Level | Beginner to Intermediate |
|---|---|
| Materials | None |
| Preparation | Decide on the questions you will use for the exercise |

Use this to review language rather than for new structures. On the board, write the first letter of every word in a question or sentence, such as: W___ i_ y___ n___? Divide students into two teams. Team A has a go at guessing the first word. If correct, they can go on to guess the second word and so on; if they guess wrongly, team B has a turn. A team keeps guessing words until they make an error, and then the other team takes over. Only the team that guesses the last word gets the point! In this case, the sentence is: What is your name? Use questions or sentences that contain grammatical structures and vocabulary that you want to review.

## Guess The Word And Variation

| Category | Spelling |
|---|---|
| Group size | Any |
| Level | Beginner to lower intermediate |
| Materials | None |
| Preparation | None |

Have a player come up to the board and write down the letters you say aloud. Take your time in between letters, as the idea is that the class has to guess what word you are spelling out. Divide the class into teams and encourage the students to call out any word at all, regardless of the fact that you may only have written one letter up so far. As an incentive, award one point for any word that could have been correct and five points for the actual correct word. If you do this, have a student keep the score so you can concentrate on the class and spelling the words. For example, if your word is 'chocolate', this starts with c, so a student who calls out 'cat' can win one point. If you have the letters ch up on the board, the word cat would no longer earn a point, but 'church' would. For an easy game, use words relating to one theme only, such as food. Use random words for intermediates with larger vocabulary. Give clues if you need to.

### Variation

Involve more people at once by making each column of people in the class a team, with one student from each team at the front by the board. The student at the front will have a series of words, say four or five, for his or her team to guess. These can all belong to a theme for beginners, but can be totally random for advanced players. The person at the front starts to write out the first word, but he or she is only allowed to write out the first four letters – then the team has to guess the word. As soon as they have guessed the word correctly, the person at the front writes out the first four letters of the second word, and so on, until all the words have been guessed.

The idea is to be the first team to guess all the words. You'll need to give out different words for each team, as the teams will hear the others calling out words. A quick way to prepare is to have each team write down five or six words for another team to guess.

## Guess Who Listening

| | |
|---|---|
| Category | Step 4 listening fluency |
| Level | Intermediate |
| Group size | Any |
| Materials | None |
| Preparation | Have information about famous people for a demonstration and then let the students prepare this for homework for the next class |

Start to talk about someone famous, or someone everyone in class knows. Give oblique facts to start out with, but gradually become more and more detailed until someone guesses whom you are talking about. Use this idea with objects as well as people.

This is a good task to set for homework. Ask each student to hand you a biographical summary of a famous person, including facts about his or her life. Use these summaries for the activity in the next lesson. Students are not allowed to guess the famous person that they researched.

With a big class, distribute the summaries and let students work in small groups to guess each other's famous person.

Shelley Ann Vernon

GAMES H–K

## Hand Sign Stories

| | |
|---|---|
| Category | Listening to learn new vocabulary |
| Group size | All class sizes |
| Level | Beginner to Intermediate |
| Materials | A vocabulary list and a text that uses these words; textbook passages, story books, articles from the web or elsewhere are all potential sources of texts |
| Preparation | Choose your text and key words to use with hand signs |

This is a great way to learn vocabulary, especially for students who show a preference for tactile learning (always moving, touching things and having difficulty retaining material they have heard or read about). Hand signs works very well with adults if you introduce them in the right way. First, go over a list of new vocabulary words and their meanings. Then ask your students to write down as many as they can remember. When you go over the ones they remembered, ask for definitions. Your students won't be able to remember very many. Then tell them that you're going to improve their recall by giving them a way to remember vocabulary and definitions more easily. Play the game as explained below.

**How to play**   First, go over the list of vocabulary words and their meanings with the class as a whole. Together, decide on a gesture or sign that will stand for the word, the funnier the better, but they should be meaningful. For example, if the word were 'nurse', you could stick your finger in your mouth like it was a thermometer. This would be a very memorable sign. The word doctor might be represented by putting your fingers in your ears with the thumbs hanging down below the face and touching under the chin like a stethoscope. A teacher could be represented by miming writing on the board.

Optionally, help your students come up with signs for abstract concepts by being open to their culture. For example, 'honesty' in the United States might be represented by raising your right hand, as if swearing on the Bible, something that Americans do in the courts. In other countries, concepts are going to be different. It's very important that students make up gestures that are significant to them, but which are the same for the whole class. Your job is to facilitate a consensus on what the hand sign for each word should be. Once you have a sign for each word, run through the list with the students a few times so that everyone is familiar with them.

Next, instruct the students to listen to a story you are going to read them and make the correct hand sign every time they hear one of the vocabulary words. If the gesture is meaningful and if the story is context rich, then students will learn the words on the vocabulary list with very little trouble. The object is to complete the story with everyone making the correct hand signs.

### *Variations*

The original is a co-operative game, but it can be competitive with teams or individuals. Thinking of it as a version of Simon Says: any student who gives the wrong sign for a word takes a point. In this game, the lowest score wins.

Alternatively, tell the story, but when you come to a vocabulary word use the hand sign only. The students call out the word based on the hand sign they see.

Another variation is, instead of coming up with the hand signs as a class, have the students work in pairs on different vocabulary items. Each pair comes up with hand signs for their words and then teaches them to the rest of the class. Then the game proceeds as usual.

Instead of a story, you could use hand signs incorporated into a role-play. Students could create a short dialogue where they use one or two words you have specified. They drill the role-play using an expressive gesture each time the given word is spoken.

For example, 'That's rubbish!' This is something we might say during an argument, so demonstrate first, imagining you are cross with someone. Tell the person, in a quite annoyed manner, that what he or she has said is rubbish, but use a gesture too. This brings the words alive, makes them stick, and give them more meaning.

At the end of the lesson or exercise, ask your students to list the vocabulary and then ask them to define the words. You'll find that their recall has improved significantly, and after this they won't have any problem with playing the game in the future.

## Higher Or Lower

| Category | Listening or speaking drill – comparatives or numbers |
|---|---|
| Group size | Flexible |
| Level | Beginner |

| Materials | Playing cards, number, picture or word cards |
|---|---|
| Preparation | Prepare the relevant word cards for comparatives |

**How to play**   If working with the whole class or one large group, turn over a number card and read the number out loud. With students divided into two teams, everyone decides whether they think the next card will be higher or lower than the previous one. Those who think it will be higher say 'higher' and point towards the ceiling. All those who think it will be lower say 'lower' and point towards the floor. Turn over the next card and read it out. Those who were wrong are out and have to sit down. Continue until you have a handful of winners.

For pair work, each pair has a pack of playing cards or number cards. One card is drawn, and each player states whether he or she thinks the next card will be higher or lower; if one player is correct, he or she keeps the card, and the idea is to collect as many cards as possible. Where there is a tie, e.g. if both players say 'higher', the card remains in a separate pile. The next time one of the pair wins a round, he or she takes the whole pile of unclaimed cards. Work with numbers by having a player read the card that is turned over each time.

## Language ideas
- Numbers and comparatives

To use higher numbers, say that each number is x10 or x100 its face value, so 6 would become 60 or 600.

This is also an ideal game for making comparative sentences, such as 'Five is higher than four,' 'Three is lower than ten' etc. You can also use 'more than', 'fewer than' (if working with countable nouns), 'less than' and 'the same as'.

- Comparative adjectives

A variant of this game is to use sets of picture or word cards. Here is an example with animals. Each time a card is turned over, the players guess whether the next animal will be bigger or smaller, or faster or slower (in real life!).

This idea could also be used with pictures of people, who can be taller, shorter, thinner, fatter, younger etc., and types of transport, which can be faster or slower.

## Homework

| Category | Step 6 writing |
|---|---|

| | |
|---|---|
| Group size | Flexible |
| Level | Beginner to advanced |
| Materials | None |
| Preparation | Prepare clear instructions for the students |

Kill two birds with one stone and use your students to prepare material for future classes through homework. For example, have your students write something that you mark. The students then bring the corrected version into class and you use the rewritten material in an activity.

Examples of games where this is a useful strategy are Anagrams, Call My Bluff Definitions, Cryptic Clues, Decision Time, Figure It Out, Gap Fill Game, Pairs, Persuasion, Questionnaires, Quiz Race, Jokes, Memory Challenge and Storytelling.

**Hot Seating**

| | |
|---|---|
| Category | Step 5 speaking fluency |
| Group size | Class divided into teams |
| Level | Intermediate to advanced |
| Materials | None |
| Preparation | Decide which words you will write on the board |

Write a selection of words on the board. Place two chairs at the front facing the students so that the people sitting down cannot see the board. A member of team A sits in one chair and one from team B in the other. The rest of team A has one minute to describe as many words as possible to their team member without mentioning the word itself, and using no gestures or drawing. Any cheating, and that team's time in the hot seat is over! The student in the hot seat names as many items as possible. Once named, these items are removed from the board. When the minute is up, team B has a turn and you alternate until all the words have been named. If possible, have two teams working at the same time with two hot seats. This way, the teams can race each other to finish describing all the words.

If you have a class of 30 you could play this with 3 teams of 10 and have all the teams playing together. Swap over the person in the hot seat for each team every couple of minutes and play until all the words have been guessed. The minute a student in the hot seat names an item on the board, a student erases it, and awards a point to that team.

Some students will hate the hot seat, being anxious at appearing a dunce in front of others. Don't force anyone to take the seat. Propose that two shy students work together in the seat to ease the pressure.

## How It's Made

| Category | Step 5 speaking fluency |
|---|---|
| Group size | This can be played in groups, or even be by a single player. The maximum number of players in a group is determined by the number of steps in the directions. Each player must have at least one step to work with, however, they can have more than one if there are more steps than players |
| Level | High beginner to advanced |
| Materials | Strips of paper or card, one with each step of the instructions written on it. The ingredients or items that need to be put together as stated in the instructions, such as puzzles or models. Variation 4 below needs no instructions |
| Preparation | Photocopied or written instructions are needed |

The purpose of this game is to work on sequencing, following directions and team co-operation.

**Preparation**   Use examples from the Appendix to demonstrate and set the task of writing instructions for others to follow for homework, in groups or individually. If any students have models or Lego sets at home, these are ideal. Photocopy the instructions (enlarge them if necessary) and chop them into chunks. Simpler models are better if you are not using pictures.

Things to build or make could range from origami, tangrams, models, Lego or puzzles to sandwiches. Give the more advanced students more steps and/or more complex instructions. Beginners need something simple, like putting the wheels on the Lego car. It's best to have one model to every three or four students to allow for plenty of speaking.

**How to play**   How it's Made simply requires directions for assembling something. It is always fun to make peanut butter sandwiches or some other simple food, and actually bring in the ingredients to work with.

The teacher hands out the strips of paper or card detailing one step of a making/building process to the players. Each player reads his or her piece of paper out loud, but cannot show it to anyone. Students discuss their step with the others and decide where they fit in. The group must try to put themselves in order so that when they read the instructions out loud again the whole thing makes sense and can be correctly followed. Then they can try to create the item.

## *Variations*

Have two groups working simultaneously, and the winner is the group that finishes first.

Have individuals sort out the order of all the strips individually; the student that finishes first wins.

Give individuals or groups a finished item and have them write out instructions for how to make it. Test their instructions by trading them with others and seeing if they work.

Another way to play this game is simply to have a rule where a student cannot move any piece without *saying* something. If a student wants to pick up a piece off the table and try it to see if it fits on the model or in the puzzle, or stick it with another piece, he or she must say something in English. For example, if tackling a puzzle with a picture that includes some red flowers, an advanced student may give a running commentary: 'I'm just going to see if this small red piece fits on here ... it looks like it might be part of a flower. Oh no, it doesn't fit.' A beginner might say, 'I think this is a flower,' or 'It fits/doesn't fit here.'

Alternatively, have students repeat any kind of sentence or grammar element that you are learning, which does not have to be related to the theme of the puzzle or model at all. A beginner could say 'I like pears' – this will give him or her the right to try a piece on the model or puzzle. If working with several groups, they can race each other to see who finishes first.

## Interviews

| | |
|---|---|
| Category | Step 5 speaking fluency |
| Level | Lower intermediate to advanced |
| Group size | Divide class in pairs or small groups |
| Materials | Interview questions |
| Preparation | Version 1: students prepare for this with homework; Version 2: no preparation |

Explain the purpose of this activity to students, which is to improve speaking fluency and interview technique, or asking and answering questions. The purpose of the activity will also depend on the type of interview that you set up and the tense you conduct most of the interview in. For example, in a job interview, candidates will be talking about themselves, their past experience and what they hope to contribute to the company and gain for themselves, so this uses a wide variety of language and tenses.

Interviews do not need to be about getting a job. They can be about anything – selecting a nutritionist to design meals for a hospital, selecting one type of environmentally sound building over another, one type of energy over another, one type of uniform over another, and so on. If you are teaching professional groups, your interviews can concern technical details relevant to the needs of your students; for example, if you teach engineers, the interview can concern their ideas for a construction project. This will motivate the students because they will feel that the activity is highly relevant to their language needs.

### *Variations*

Version 1 – written homework as preparation
Give the students the task of preparing interview questions for homework. Mark these questions beforehand if you wish. Students then bring their questions into class and take turns interviewing each other. Students can interview several other students and select a candidate for the job/requirement from those interviewed.

Version 2 – in-class writing and speaking activity
Use this activity with any type of interview. The example given here is suitable for beginners to lower intermediates and concerns describing and talking about people.

**How to play**    First, students think about a famous person who they would like to meet and write that person's name at the top of a piece of paper. Students leave their papers on their desks and mill around, looking at the other suggestions and writing questions that they would like to know about the famous person on the sheet.

Allow up to 10 minutes for this, during which time the teacher can be on hand to help students form their questions or correct any written errors. Then have all students return to their desks and read the questions written for them by others. Finally, students pair up and interview each other about their chosen famous people, using the questions others have written on their paper.

## I Took A Trip

| Category | Step 2 speaking drill – past tense question forms |
|---|---|
| Level | Beginner |
| Group size | Divide class into small groups |
| Materials | None |
| Preparation | None |

Start by saying, 'I took a trip. What did I take with me?' The group members each name an item such as a t-shirt, a suitcase, a book, your dog etc. Next, ask 'What did I wear around my neck?' Students always give the same answer, regardless of the question, which leads to incongruities. If anyone laughs or smiles at an answer, he or she does a forfeit.

Continue asking questions such as 'What did I eat?' 'What did I photograph?' 'What did I take swimming?' Play another round and let the students think up questions to ask.

## Jeopardy

| Category | Step 2 speaking drill or fluency activity |
|---|---|
| Group size | 2 to 20 students. With 2 to 4 students, play individually; with more students, put them into teams of 4 |
| Level | Beginner to advanced |
| Materials | Jeopardy board from the Appendix for small groups or use the board |
| Preparation | Questions for the grammar or topic you are studying, which the students can prepare for homework |

This game reviews previously taught information, works on questions and answers with structured team interaction, and builds team skills.

**Preparation**    Jeopardy is based on a popular American quiz game. It takes a little preparation the first time you play, but once you've made up a set of questions you can keep them for future use. You'll need a Jeopardy board, either by printing the one from the Appendix, or by drawing one on the board.

If you are using the classroom board, you will need 25 envelopes and at least 30 cards (5 category cards, and 25 question cards) that fit into the envelopes. Write your five categories across the top of the board. Now, stick up the envelopes in a 5 x 5 pattern with a column under each category card, as shown in the diagram. (Cut off the envelope flaps so that they make open pockets to hold question cards.) On the envelopes, write the number of points each question is worth: the first row is 50; the second is 75; the third is 125; the fourth is 200 points; the fifth is 500. The more difficult the question, the more points it is worth. This is your Jeopardy

| Vocabulary | Tenses | Question Forms | Irregular Verbs | General |
|---|---|---|---|---|
| One envelope stuck in each grid with question card inside | 50 points | 50 points | 50 points |  |
| 75 points | 75 points | 75 points | 75 points | 75 points |
| 125 points | 125 points | 125 points | 125 points | 125 points |
| 200 points | 200 points | 200 points | 200 points | 200 points |
| 500 points | 500 points | 500 points | 500 points | 500 points |

board made up.

If you are using small boards for table-top games and your students are working in small groups, use the Jeopardy board and blank cards from the Appendix.

Next, you need topics and related questions. For these, choose topics you have already covered, as this will ensure that students are familiar with the answers needed – for beginners, you might use clothing, sports, food, the weather and countries, topics such as nouns, verbs, adjectives, prepositions and adverbs, or pop music, fashion, movie and fiction. If you have business students, you might include business-related topics. Choose topics that interest your students! The best way to ensure this is to ask the students to give you the topics and to prepare a range of questions, with answers, for homework. This means that you obtain interesting questions that are highly relevant to your group without being an expert yourself. Collect a host of questions from the students and make a selection from them for the actual game.

Questions can be created to fit the level of your class. A beginner's grammar question might be something like 'Is the word *run* a noun or a verb?' (answer: both!), 'I run, you run, he or she ...' (runs) or What is the future tense of 'We go to the cinema'? (We will go to the cinema, or We are going to the cinema later). Questions about vocabulary should ask for spelling, definitions or to use the word in a sentence. In an advanced adult class, you might want to include cultural questions, such as polite greetings and responses, or how to answer the phone.

**How to play**     This game can be played with as few as two people and as many as twenty. With two to four students, each can play individually, otherwise put the students into teams of three or four and allow them to take turns selecting their questions. The teacher may decide who goes first. The first student selects a category. He or she must answer the first available question within the category. If he or she answers correctly, he or she earns the points as indicated on the envelope; if wrongly, another team may attempt to answer the question. If no one can answer the question correctly, then the teacher explains the answer and no one gets the points.

### *Variations*

Allow students to pick from any pocket on the board. They may choose harder questions worth more points earlier, in this case. This will affect strategy and may encourage more discussion among team members about the best way to proceed. If your students work well together, this is a good alternative.

Play this game in the same way as the original Jeopardy: write *answers* on the cards, and have the students phrase questions that fit in order to win points. This is a great way to work on question formats, but it works best with a higher-level group. The winner is the team with the most points once all the questions are answered.

### Jigsaw Listening

| | |
|---|---|
| Category | Step 4 listening fluency |
| Group size | Divide the class into small groups |
| Level | Beginner to intermediate |
| Materials | An audio recording or a passage to read out, plus the same passage written down |
| Preparation | You will need one chopped-up copy of passage you will work with per group |

Give students the jumbled sentences of a reading passage. For beginners, chop the sentences up whole; for more advanced students, chop the sentences randomly. One strip of paper may include the end of one sentence and the start of another. Then read out or play the passage, and tell students they will only be able to hear the passage two/three times. Let students listen in groups to the passage read out at normal speed and work out the order of the sentences.

### Variation

Play as above, but give each student one strip of paper that he or she is responsible for inserting it into the order. Students cannot show their paper to others, as this task has to be done through listening, not reading.

## Joker

| Category | Step 2 speaking drill |
|---|---|
| Group size | Divide class into small groups |
| Level | Beginner to lower intermediate |
| Materials | Playing cards and questions for the students to answer |
| Preparation | Prepare one set of questions per group |

Deal out half a pack of playing cards, including the jokers, to a small group of up to six students. The players must not look at their cards but place them face down on the table. Ask player 1 a question. Player 1 answers and turns over a playing card from his or her pile. If the answer is correct, the card is taken out of the game. If the answer is incorrect, the card is placed in a pile in the middle of the group. Continue by asking the next student a question. When the joker turns up, the person who turned it over must collect all the discarded cards from the pile in the middle, *unless* he or she has answers the question correctly, in which case the joker is taken out of the game. You may like to add in a couple of extra jokers from another pack.

　　If you have six students or fewer, play as described above. With a larger class, split the students into groups, and either give a set of questions on a sheet of A4 to each group leader, who takes the questions in order, or print out the questions on card and chop up in advance. The teacher circulates and helps out where needed.

**Language ideas**　　Use any question forms you like. Use the same question form over and over for a lower level or mix up various types of questions for revision games or for more advanced levels.

**Jokes**

| Category | Step 5 speaking fluency |
|---|---|
| Group size | Any |
| Level | Lower intermediate to advanced |
| Materials | Jokes such as those at the end of this book, and those your students give you. Ignore any unsuitable jokes that may be offensive. Jokes are often culturally sensitive, so please use with caution |
| Preparation | Ask each student to submit a few jokes to you for homework and use those in class for this activity |

Explain to the students that this is a speaking fluency activity in which they will tell short stories, because jokes are really stories. Distribute one joke to each student and let students read and rehearse their jokes in their heads. Ideally, have a different joke per student.

When students are ready, let them pair up and tell each other their jokes from memory. Every two minutes, depending on the length of jokes you have handed out, students swap partners. At the end, ask students which jokes were actually funny, and see if anyone wants to translate a joke from their own language.

GAMES L–M

## Last Card

| | |
|---|---|
| Category | Step 2 speaking drill |
| Level | Beginner to lower intermediate |
| Group size | Divide class into small groups of 3 to 4 students |
| Materials | A large quantity of small picture or word flashcards |
| Preparation | None |

Each group of students has a stack of about 15 flashcards, which are laid out in a grid. Rows can be uneven and contain any number of cards. You may have the first row with four cards, the second with three, the third with five, the fourth with two, and so on. Cards are face up. Students may remove any number of cards from a given row per turn. To remove a card, the student has to name the vocabulary (use picture flashcards) or use a word in a sentence (use picture or word flashcards). The sentence may be of a fixed structure for grammar drill or freer to encourage fluency. The player who takes the last card loses.

For complete beginners, play this game with the alphabet – the player who takes the z loses. Equally, play with numbers, and designate which number will be the losing number at the start of the game.

## Lego Negotiations

| | |
|---|---|
| Category | Speaking fluency or drill as required |
| Level | Flexible levels; drill-type communication for beginners repeating the same phrases or freer communication for more advanced |
| Group | Ideally, groups of three |
| Materials | Either use Lego, tangrams (geometric shapes cut in card or foam) or blocks. Pictures of the finished designs made with the available shapes, one for each group |
| Preparation | Initial preparation time is 30 to 60 minutes, but, once done, you don't have to do it again. Collect your Lego or blocks, |

> or cut out your tangrams. Make sure you have enough so that each group can construct a design. You need a picture of the finished design

This game was developed from a game that uses ingredients, and it can be played this way as a variation. The general object of the game is to collect all the items you need to complete a project: in this case, a figure made of Lego bricks, blocks, or tangrams. The objective is to develop negotiation language at whatever level is suitable for your students.

**How to play**    The main version of this game uses language that is very simple: 'Do you have a red (colour) triangle (shape)?'

Pre-teach the language needed, and drill the sentence starters as a group. With beginners and intermediates, use a game like Relay Race to drill the negotiation sentences to be sure they are fluent before playing.

Then distribute the pieces among the groups, with three students in each. Hand out a picture of the design that the group has to build. The students then take turns asking other groups for certain pieces that they need to complete their design.

If a group has the piece asked for, they must give it up. If they don't have it, then the next group gets a turn to ask someone. The first group to complete their design is the winner.

### *Variation*

In this variation, the language objective becomes more complex, as does the strategy. Students could ask: 'Do you have a green (colour) square (shape)?' 'May I have it?' 'I will give you the green square if you can give me a blue circle.'

Pre-teach the language needed, and drill the sentence starters as a group. This is key to this game's effectiveness. Then distribute the pieces among the groups, with three students in each. Hand out the picture of the design that the group has to build.

The students take turns asking other groups for certain pieces that they need to complete their design. If the group has a piece another group needs, then they have to negotiate and trade for it. If the group doesn't have a piece the other group wants, then they can try to trade with another group to get it.

It is best to keep the groups separate enough that the negotiations can't be easily overheard.

*Change the language to make this game more or less formal. It's a good idea to play the game at different levels of formality, especially with business English students. It helps to point out the contrast between 'Will you give me the red triangle, please?' and 'Would you be interested in exchanging this blue square for the red triangle?'*

*You can find tangrams by searching online. You can also buy 3D sets in toy stores. Here is an example:*

## Lyrics and Songs – Ten Ideas for Using Songs in Class

| | |
|---|---|
| Category | Step 4 fluency listening and/or Step 6 creative writing |
| Level | Beginner to upper intermediate |
| Group size | Any |
| Materials | A song and optional lyrics sheet written out with gaps |
| Preparation | Selecting a suitable song and putting the lyrics in a word document to edit them for the activities below. There are websites with words already typed up that can be copied and pasted |

Find a song with lyrics suitable for your class level. With beginners, use a pop song – just take the chorus if the verses are too difficult. Look for songs that are decent in terms of content, and at medium tempo. Slower songs can be hard to understand and you do not want students sitting around during lots of 'ooohs' and 'ahhhs'. Avoid songs with instrumental solos so as not to waste valuable class time. Avoid rap, which is usually too fast and incomprehensible even to native speakers, not to mention politically incorrect.

**How to play**   Preferably, use a song that is not well known, but has clear lyrics. Often lone artists are easier to understand than a rock band. Folk and country songs often work well, as lyrics are a big part of them. Write

10 to 15 words that feature in the song on pieces of paper and stick them to the board. If you have a big class, you'll need to do this in groups at tables, and make one set of words per group. With 15 students or fewer playing in teams, the board is fine.

Put the students into two or three teams, lined up before the board, and play the song. When a word on the board is sung the front line of students race to grab the relevant paper from the board (or table top if playing in groups). Those students now go to back of the line so that other students have a turn. Let the song run continuously until all words are taken.

## *Variations*

**Cloze Passages**     The students listen to a song and fill in the gaps. www.lyrics.com has videos and lyrics that can be copied and pasted into word, so it's easy to make your gap fill.

**Dictation**     Students listen and write out the lyrics themselves as a dictation. If doing this, it is recommended to have them work in pairs or small groups to help each other out.

**Story writing**   Let students listen to the song once or twice and then get together in groups and tell the story of the song, or write it out in note form. American country songs are good for this, as they usually have a story.

**Jumbled sentences**     Give students the lyrics in jumbled sentences. Let students listen in groups and work out the sentences.

**Jigsaw listening**     Give students all the song lyrics on pieces of paper, one line of lyrics per paper. Play the song twice and let students reorder the sentences. A variant is that students cannot show their lyrics to the others – everything has to be done through listening.

**Use of words**   Let students listen to a song and count up the number of times certain words are used, or the superlative form or how many adjectives they hear, and so on.

**Discussion**     Play a song to the students once or twice and then discuss it. What is the song about? Is the singer right? Would you feel the same way? What would you do in this situation? If you have a large class, let students discuss questions you provide in groups. Let students come up with their own questions about the song to ask each other.

**Creative writing** Have the students make up another verse or chorus for the song – if they are willing, they can even sing it to the others. If they do not want to sing just let them read it out. Most adults are pretty self-conscious when it comes to singing in front of others, but they might join in if singing in a group.

Alternatively, use a familiar tune and let students put lyrics, using text from your textbook or current vocabulary and grammar. For example, take a Beatles tune or well-known movie theme put day-to-day language to it. For example, take The Beatles' 'All You Need is Love'. Students get together in groups and write new words based on describing their day.

'Brush, brush, brush, wash, wash, wash, brush, brush, brush, it's easy!
Every day I brush my teeth.
Every day I wash my face.
Every day I put on my clothes, it's easy!
All you need is a sink, da da da da da.
All you need is some soap, da da da da da.
All you need are some clothes, yeah, that is all you need.'

It's fun, and quite creative and useful.

## Mad Libs

| | |
|---|---|
| Category | Parts of speech review and Step 4 listening for fluency |
| Group size | One or more divided into groups of up to ten per group |
| Level | Intermediate to advanced |
| Materials | A sheet of paper with a passage with blanks to fill in |
| Preparation | None with the store bought version or make your own |

This game is based on a popular American game. It takes some preparation initially, but can be played with minimal resources. Use it to review parts of speech: nouns, verbs, adjectives, adverbs, prepositions and so on.

Make a gap fill from any textbook or book, or create one. Decide what parts of speech you want to review and delete these from the passage, keeping a copy of the original. Make the blanks big enough to write in. Use a current reading passage from your textbook, a short story, or a text covered a few weeks ago that you want to review. An easy way to do this is to photocopy the written page and use whitener to paint over the words you want to delete. If you take a scan of that page (or copy it again), you will have a blank template to use for future classes.

**How to play**   Hold the paper with the reading and the blanks and do not let the students see it. Explain to the students that you are going to ask them for different parts of speech and they need to give you a word that is a good example of this. You might need to give an example or go over the different parts of speech. Ask a student for a word by saying, 'Give me an example of a noun/verb/adjective/adverb' etc. Write down the student's response in the relevant blank, but don't read anything yet. Continue around the room until all the blanks in the story are filled. Now read the story out loud – generally, there will be much laughter. This works well when you use a familiar text.

### *Variations*

Allow students to work in teams and award points for words that fit the part of speech you asked for. In this case, the winner has the most points. Or, have a student take your role, ask for the parts of speech and read the story at the end.

Another option is to have students vote on the funniest sentence from the story. Compare it with the original and discuss the differences.

Students could also write out a number of sentences and delete the required part of speech. Students then swap papers and circulate, asking other students for a part of speech to go in each gap. Once all the sentences are completed, students get into groups and read through all the sentences. The group with the most sentences that actually make sense, as opposed to being nonsense, wins. This could generate some lively debate about what is nonsense and what is not.

## Make A Sentence Or A Question

| | |
|---|---|
| Category | Step 2 speaking drill |
| Group size: | Two players to a class |
| Level | Beginner to advanced |
| Materials | None |
| Preparation | None |

**How to play**    Divide your group into teams and call a word out loud, or have a class member do it. The teams race to come up with a sentence or question containing that word. Other teams decide if it is correct. Teams earn points for producing correct sentences and also for marking them correctly. Do this orally, as writing will slow the whole exercise down. Use time limits to keep the pace moving. If you notice that one team is way ahead, move some of the better students over to even things out. To avoid one student giving all the answers, allow one answer per student, and let the better students help the others out if necessary.

**Language Ideas**    Use English in a general way or be specific about what you drill. To focus on a specific linguistic structure, specify that a sentence must be in a certain tense, or use a certain phrase. This game is adaptable to any language at all and is useful for drilling new structures or ironing out consistent errors. Here is a simple version and a complex one.

- Beginner's example

Name different foods. The students make up sentences or questions about whether they like or dislike them. Or hold up a picture or word and say 'sentence' or 'question'. The class or team must come up with a response. For example, you hold up a picture of the word 'ice-cream' and then say 'Question.' The students must think of questions containing the word, such as 'Do you like ice-cream?' 'Can I have some ice-cream please?' 'Is there any ice-cream?'

- Intermediate to advanced example

To drill if + past perfect with the perfect conditional, you could say the sentence must contain a phrase such as 'If I had wanted ...'

If the given word is mother, the player needs to make up a sentence such as 'If I had wanted mother to do it I would have asked her.'

If the word named is pancake, a sentence could be 'If I had wanted a pancake, I would have asked for it.' Likewise, for tiger, 'If I had wanted to see a tiger, I would have gone to India.' And so on.

**Making Up Stories**

| | |
|---|---|
| Category | Step 5 speaking fluency and writing |
| Group size | Divide the class into small groups |
| Level | Beginner to advanced |
| Materials | None |

| Preparation | Choose your opening story line, final line or random words that must be included in the story |
|---|---|

**How to play**          Put your class into small groups – the smaller the better – and have them make up a story that they write as they go, using a series of random pictures or words. You may choose to instruct students to make the story plausible despite the disparate elements they must draw from to write it. They will enjoy the challenge of making up a story using their imaginations rather than following the often dull and obvious storylines of picture composition prompts provided in textbooks of old.

You may wish to give the opening line, or a final line, or a certain number of words that must be included in the story to stimulate the students' imaginations.

Examples of opening lines might be:
- He should never have gone there.
- I peered into the dark hole.
- Today is the most important day of my life.

Examples of closing lines might be:
- There was nothing for me to do but cry.
- Luckily, I still had the coin in my pocket.

For lower intermediates, provide easier sentences such as:
- It's a fish.
- Today I take the train to London.

**Language and marking**          You may need to encourage intermediate students to keep it simple, as the temptation will be to try to write an incredible story, but they will not yet have the necessary language and grammar to do so. You may want to give them the tense the story takes place in – for example, it was yesterday, it is happening now, or it is someone telling story about what they plan to do in the future.

Once students have written the story, have them pass their story to the next group, who must correct any language mistakes they see by writing out the correct version beneath the story. Then pass the stories on again, and each time the story is passed to another group they add any corrections they feel necessary. As far as the corrections go, you may have several versions offered, so go through any such queries with students, reading out the different versions and having the class say which one is correct.

You won't need to read out all the stories, as students will have read them (or some of them), and depending on your class size you might not want to correct absolutely everything in this way. However, having students participate in the marking of work makes them focus on the details such as verb endings and those little prepositions that are so often wrong.

This is a great exercise in awareness, and saves you marking 30-odd stories to boot! If possible, make yourself available to individuals who may want to clarify things with you as a result of this exercise. If you cannot stay for a few minutes after class, then see people individually, briefly, while the other students do a written task or some group work.

## Marooned

| | |
|---|---|
| Category | Step 5 speaking fluency |
| Group size | Split the class into groups |
| Level | Intermediate to advanced |
| Materials | None |
| Preparation | Decide on the scenario that will be discussed. |

Divide your class into teams. Your students are marooned on an island. What five or six items would they want with them, and why? Let students discuss this question and come to a group consensus. (It's five items per *team*, not per person!) Then pair students from different groups so they can compare what another group has chosen to take and why. Use this idea again during different lessons to discuss other subjects, such as:

- If you could only listen to one type of music, which would it be, and why?
- Which animal would you bring to a deserted island, and why?
- Which five types of food would you bring, and why?
- Which four things would you change in your life, and why?

If some of your students are shy or do not feel comfortable talking about themselves in such a personal way, use a third party. For example, which four things would you change about your life if you were the Queen of England/the President of the USA/an actor, and why?

## Match Up

| | |
|---|---|
| Category | Step 2 speaking drill or Step 5 speaking fluency |
| Group size | Small group to a class |

| Level | Beginner to advanced |
|---|---|
| Materials | Pictures or words on pieces of paper |
| Preparation | Prepare a list of matching items |

Think of pairs of words that go together, such as hair and hairbrush, and find pictures of both, or make two word flashcards. Once you have enough pairs, shuffle, and hand out one card per player in your group or class. Players must keep their cards hidden and find their other half by walking about the classroom asking the other students verbal questions. Showing your picture or word to another student is cheating – everything must be done orally.

With complete beginners, give out identical pairs of pictures so they can match dog with dog, for example. This allows you to work on basic vocabulary. Players can just name the item that they have and see if it matches the other player's item. Or players can ask a simple question such as 'What have you got?' They reply with a sentence such as 'I've got a book.'

For an intermediate version, players can say one sentence about their item as a clue – for example, 'You use it to tidy your hair.' Students circle the room saying their sentence to the other players until they find their partners.

For the advanced version, players must guess whether the other item matches theirs by asking questions about it. They are not allowed to name their items and miming is not allowed. Students must talk about the item they have and then listen to the other person describing his or her item to see if there is a match.

*Match professions with tools needed for a certain job – a doctor with a stethoscope, pliers with an electrician, buttons with a tailor and megaphone with film director (somewhat more cryptic!) and so on.*

*You can also use this idea with the riddles, jokes and metaphors at the end of this book. Split the metaphors in half, the riddle into the statement and the answer, or separate the punchline from the joke. Add some excitement to the game by specifying that the first five people to find a match are winners – after that, the game stops.*

## *Variation*

Students write down one of their hobbies on a piece of paper and pass it to the front. The teacher draws a grid with student names down the left and hobbies across the top. Students intermingle, asking each other questions about their hobbies and filling in the grid on the board. If you have a larger class, ask them instead to find another student who shares the same interest.

## Memory Challenge

| | |
|---|---|
| Category | Step 2 speaking drill/fluency |
| Group size | Any, working in pairs |
| Level | Beginner to lower intermediate |
| Materials | Class board |
| Preparation | Decide on the information you will write in the grid or have students prepare something for homework |

The teacher writes some information in a grid on the board. While he or she is doing this, the students are reading and attempting to remember the information. An example of a grid to enable beginners to talk about people would show names down the left hand side of the board and characteristics across the top. For example:

| John | married to Sylvia | works as an engineer | likes tennis and dancing | dislikes rock climbing |
|---|---|---|---|---|
| Mary | single | works as a part-time cleaner | likes chess | dislikes getting up early |
| Sylvia | married to John | works as a nurse | likes dancing and watching soap operas | dislikes tennis |

Next, bring a student up to the front and have him or her face away from the board. Ask him or her questions about the content on the board, such as, 'Is John married?' 'What's Sylvia's job?' and so on. The student answers from memory as best as he or she can. Let students ask some questions too. Once everyone knows what to do, divide the class into pairs or very small groups and let them continue to play, swapping over the person who answers the questions without looking at the board every five questions.

This idea can be used to work on different tenses or grammatical points. For example, use headers in the grid that refer to the past or the future, such as what the person did yesterday, what he or she is doing later today, how long he or she has done a certain hobby or job, what he or she would do if any job in the world, and so on.

Use this same idea to test real content, not just dull, invented facts about imaginary people. The above examples about people will be more interesting if you use class members, pop stars or famous people as subjects on the board. Another idea is to use Trivial Pursuit-type questions and write facts and figures on the board. For example, you might write facts about different movies, when they were made, who starred in them, the budget to make them and the amount they grossed at the box office. Or you might choose world records, facts about the body, or information about famous businesspeople. Use themes that are of interest and relevant to your students' needs. Set the fact finding for homework and give each student a topic to research; then use their homework for class.

Most adults will find participating in this game, or a version of it, fulfilling because they will be learning new information and testing their memory skills as well as using their English. Write your facts, such as Mumbai is the largest city in the world with a population of 14 million people, on the board, and then elicit questions as part of your demonstration, such as: 'What is the largest city in the world?' 'What is the population of the largest city in the world?' 'How many people live in Mumbai?' Then let the students work in pairs. (NB too few facts, and the game will be too easy!) With beginners, use similar 'types' of facts so the question forms will not be too diverse. To make this game a drill, use identical kinds of facts so that students drill the same question form each time.

**Mind Mapping**

| | |
|---|---|
| Category | Vocabulary game |
| Group size | Any |
| Level | Beginner to intermediate |
| Materials | None |
| Preparation | None |

Each student starts with a blank piece of paper. In the middle, each writes something down, for example a noun, adjective or short sentence. If you have the time, ask students to illustrate the word or sentence briefly with a small sketch. Next, students swap papers with someone. Students draw a spoke out from the central item and add something that they feel is associated with it. Papers are then passed on again. This process continues until the mind maps are filled up.

If you are able, display these on the walls for students to browse. This activity helps students remember vocabulary because they associate it to other words.

Another way to mind map might be as follows. The teacher starts by drawing a mind map, which could be of his or her life. So it might have the teacher in the middle, then stick figures for family members, or friends, or pets, his or her work place and other elements of his or her life outside of work – holidays, hobbies, home and garden, likes, dislikes, sports and so on. Students then ask questions about the map in order to understand the content. Let students do this with each other in pairs.

A mind map could be used as the basis of a story, or to work on giving off-the-cuff presentations using a map drawn by a fellow student.

A beginner's mind map might look like this:

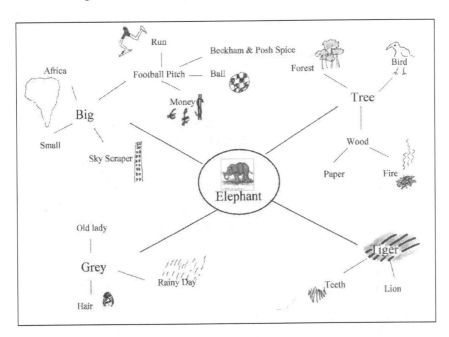

### Variation

Use a mind map created by one of your students. Divide the class into teams of 3–5 and give each student a number. All the 1s then come out to the front, have a minute to look at the mind map and then return to their tables and draw/reproduce what they remember. Numbers 2s then come out, look at the mind map and return to their group to add to the image.

This would work with any vocabulary themes, e.g. a diagram of a house with furniture/rooms/objects labelled, a map with names of countries in English, animals, food, clothing etc.

**Mine Sweep**

| Category | Step 2 speaking drill – vocabulary and short sentences |
|---|---|
| Group size | Divide into small groups of six maximum |
| Level | Beginner to lower intermediate |
| Materials | Picture or word flashcards |
| Preparation | None |

Divide the class into small groups of four to six players. Each group has two teams of two or three players each. Give a pack of picture or word flashcards to each group. Designate one word or picture to be the mine. If you are teaching students who might be upset by the idea of mines, change the name of the game and use a burst balloon idea. The first student turns over a card in the pack rapidly and names the vocabulary item, or says a short sentence with the word in it. The sentence must be correct – the other team is responsible for picking up any errors. If correct, the student keeps the card for his or her team, making one point. An error means no point.

The game continues like this until a student picks out a 'mine' card. This means that the team has to give up three of their cards, which are returned to the main pack at the bottom or taken out of the game, as you prefer. When the pack is finished, students can count up the team points and see who won, if they like.

Use picture cards with beginners or when studying vocabulary. Word cards are fine to use for revising spelling of known vocabulary and when making sentences.

**Movies – Using Previews And Excerpts**

| Category | Listening and speaking fluency |
|---|---|
| Group size | Any |
| Level | Intermediate to advanced |
| Materials | The ability to show movies or clips in class |
| Preparation | Select suitable previews or picking out quotes from movies |

Showing a long movie during class time is not constructive – watching a film is something students can do in their free time. If you survey your students, you will probably find that they do not want to be stuck in front of a film during class time either, unless they are on some kind of intensive course and need a break.

Movies can be used constructively, though, and can be brilliant learning tools. Loaning suitable films out to your students that they can watch outside of class time, preferably without subtitles, benefits them hugely, as watching movies gives exposure to natural language in a non-threatening environment. If you cannot find films without subtitles, urge your students not to use them, or change them to English, as this can help comprehension and keeps the students thinking in English rather than in their own language. Films also provide something for students of all cultures to talk about.

Needless to say, one should be cautious when selecting films to recommend or use in class. While no one bats an eyelid at partial nudity in the USA, this is shocking and disgusting in many other countries. Many adaptations of classic literature – Dickens, Jane Austen or the Brontë sisters – are suitable, as they contain neither swearing nor nudity, and very little violence, if any. Walt Disney cartoons will generally be a safe bet too.

## Movie Game 1 – Guess The Dialogue
In class, use movies constructively by showing excerpts without sound and let the students guess what the dialogue is about in each case. Then have students make up their own dialogues in pairs, or in groups, corresponding to the amount of people talking in the clip.

## Movie Game 2 – Role-Play The Dialogues
Students listen to the audio track of a movie excerpt and then in groups act this out as a role-play. The groups perform their versions to the class before watching the actual clip with its original soundtrack. This activity is best if you hand out the script in advance, so students can learn their words for homework and come back to class to rehearse and perform.

## Movie Game 3 – Preview Game
Show a preview to a movie and let the class members write in note form what they think happens in the film. For lower levels, show the film with sound. For intermediates, show the clip without sound; for advanced students, let them hear the sound, but not see the picture. Students can discuss potential movie plots and outcomes in groups and then present

their versions to the class. Finish by watching the preview again and then, if you have it, by showing a clips of the film itself.

### Movie Game 4 – Work Out The Plot

Show the opening two or three minutes of a film. Sometimes a film has a series of scenes that occur before the credits roll, so show that. Next, jump forward to the next chapter or scene, and show 10 to 20 seconds. Do this for up to five scenes. Students then get together in pairs to work out the plot of the movie together. Once most students have finished this task, put them into groups of four, and let each pair tell the other pair their version and choose a plot and an outcome to present to the rest of the class. If time allows, the class vote on which summary they think is the best.

Finish by showing the last two or three minutes of the film so students have resolution, or make the film available for students to borrow and watch in their free time. Vary the difficulty of the activity by showing only the picture, with no sound, or just the sound with no picture.

### Movie Game 5 – Using Previews For Discussion

Show your students a selection of three to five previews. Put the students in pairs to discuss which film they would like to see in full and why. To encourage more talking, ask students to list the three films in order of preference, saying why each time. Students can also try to convince their partner to come and see the film of their choice by telling them what it's about and why they think it would be good.

### Movie Game 6 – Directors And Ticket Buyers

Using the idea in the game Persuasion in this book, have students watch a movie from a selection of films for homework. Offer a choice of five films and insist, if possible, that the films be watched in English without subtitles, or at least with English subtitles. If this is not practical for you, then ask the class to think of some movies they have seen. Take these films and make five students film directors who have to sell tickets for their film. The students listen in groups to the directors and ask questions about the film if necessary. Each group of students visits each director for a few minutes. Then individuals decide which film they would go and see based on what they have learned about the films from the directors.

At the end, count up, and see who managed to sell the most tickets. It is better if not all students have seen all the movies. This way, the directors have more reason to talk about and describe their film. You might find that picking some films just released works well, as not all students will have been to see them. This is better than picking a well-known, classic film that almost everyone has already seen.

## Movie Game 7 – Listening For Quotes
Play some movie previews and give students a list of quotes from them, in random order. Students listen and write the film title by the quote. Alternatively, show five minutes of a film with dense dialogue and provide a list of quotes from it. Show the clip again and while listening students identify who says each quote.

Use a clip taken from any part of a film that contains several characters and plenty of dialogue. Adaptations of plays are full of suitable material for this activity.

## Movie Game 8 – Match The Title To The Film
Write a series of film titles on the board, perhaps 10 to 15. Show three previews and ask students to decide in pairs which titles from the board go with the previews and why. Students then present their arguments to other students in small groups, explaining why they have decided to match a certain title to a preview. Specify that to prevent one student from doing all the speaking everyone in the group must say something, and have a rule that if a student has explained a match for one film he or she cannot have a second turn – someone else must take over.

Finally, have a vote and see what the class consensus is; then give the actual titles to the three previews.

## Movie Game 9 – Watchers And Listeners
Send half of the students out with 15 to 20 key words from 5 previews, which you have prepared beforehand. These students are to make sure they understand all of the vocabulary and look them up terms in a dictionary if not. Meanwhile, play the previews to the students in the room, without sound. Then send these 'watchers' out of the room to discuss in pairs what the plots of the five movies are about and what they think happens at the end.

Meanwhile, the 'listeners' come back into the room. Play the five previews to them with no picture and only sound. Allow a few minutes for students to get together in pairs and decide what the five movies are about. Now, bring in the watchers, and put one watcher with one listener in pairs. Let them take turns describing the movies that they either heard or saw to each other and between them decide on a title for each of the movies. If there is time, play the previews again with sound and pictures so the students can assess the accuracy of their summaries.

### Movie Game 10 – Creative Writing Or Role-Play

Students write a short play based on a well-known movie (or book/story). This could be a one-person show or group work with two or more students. Try different combinations of group/individual for variety throughout the term. The fun and challenge of this game is to condense an entire film, play, book or story down into two minutes of talking time. Acting or gestures should be obligatory in order to encourage students to be creative and gain confidence expressing themselves. Even if students are stilted initially, over time, as they become used to fully participating in your classes, they will loosen up and develop.

You might want to demonstrate this task first so that is clear, but if you are fearful of demonstrating don't let this stop you from using the idea. Ask for a volunteer instead. The more well-known your story, the easier this will be, but bear in mind that the story must be well known to your *students*, not to you.

A very shy student who refuses to join in might take the task of script writer or prompt, if the group is performing from memory. Either way, just being in the class while the activity goes on will help that person learn through absorption. You can't force people to join in – this may be counter-productive.

### Mystery Game

| | |
|---|---|
| Category | Speaking fluency |
| Group size | Divide into small groups |
| Level | Intermediate to advanced |
| Materials | Objects and a bag |
| Preparation | None |

Tell students that this is a speaking fluency activity through describing things, which also leads to vocabulary expansion. Place a mystery object in a bag and give it to a student to feel and describe. The class listens to the description and tries to guess the object inside the bag. Intermediate students will find this quite difficult, as a large amount of vocabulary is needed for the task.

You might do two or three demonstrations and then ask the students to go away and prepare by each selecting three objects and looking up all the useful adjectives to describe that object. Students then bring their object into class, hidden in bags, and you play again, in small groups, with students taking it in turns to guess an object in a bag. Students describing the object should not know what it is and so should not describe their own. The teacher should have all the objects hidden so that they can be swapped over without the students seeing. If this class is too big to play this as a whole, let a group leader be in charge for objects in his or her group.

The winners can be the students who bring in objects that nobody can guess.

GAMES N–P

## Name the Thing

| | |
|---|---|
| Category | Step 5 speaking fluency |
| Group size | Any size working in pairs or small groups |
| Level | Lower intermediate to advanced |
| Materials | Pictures, which students can prepare |
| Preparation | None |

This game requires sets of picture cards. Have the students work in pairs, and lay out for each pair a set of three or four pictures of similar, but not identical, items, such as four similar cars. One of the pair holds a matching picture to one of those displayed on the table, and uses this as a reference for answering questions asked by the other student.

These students ask questions to narrow down their choices and pick the correct matching picture. The more advanced students could do the questioning, as this is harder than coming up with answers.

*A tip for this game is to first demonstrate it and then ask students to each collect a set of pictures to use in the next lesson. The teacher can then keep the best of those sets for future use.*

## No 'Yes' or 'No'

| | |
|---|---|
| Category | Step 2 speaking drill – good for questions and short-form answers |
| Group size | Small groups |
| Level | High beginner to intermediate |
| Materials | None |
| Preparation | Think of the topics students will ask questions about and prepare examples |

One student comes up into the 'hot seat' at the front or in the middle of the room. The other students ask a barrage of questions to the student at the front, who must answer them without using 'yes' or 'no'. The minute the student in the hot seat accidentally lets slip a 'yes' or 'no', or makes an error, he or she must give the place up to someone else. This encourages the use of short-form answers such as 'I do' instead of 'yes' or 'I haven't' instead of 'no'. Review short-form answers before playing by brainstorming with the class. Point out that the correct short-form answer is contained in the question. 'Have you been to Paris?' 'I have.'/'I have not.' 'Did you see a movie?' 'I did.'/'I did not.' 'Could you eat the whole steak?' 'I could.'/'I could not.' And so on.

This game is excellent for drilling questions. With beginners, students can stick to basic questions, which can be highly repetitive – 'Do you like jam?' 'I do.' 'Do you like apples?' 'I do.' 'Do you like sugar?' 'I do not.' You may play in a freer way with more advanced students who have more language and vocabulary under their belts, or you may stick to playing with a specific question form in order to drill it thoroughly.

Students may score points for each question answered correctly. Equally, you may set a fixed time limit in the hot seat to ensure everyone has a turn and score points for all correct answers given during that time. Alternatively, you do not need to keep score, but just give each student a chance to answer a set number of questions. If you have too many students to do this, then let four or five students have a turn, and play again in another lesson with different people in the hot seat.

**Noughts (Zeros) and Crosses**

| Category | Step 2 speaking drill |
|---|---|
| Group size | Pair work |
| Level | Beginner to lower intermediate |
| Materials | Pictures or questions written on the board or handed out |
| Preparation | None |

Put the students in pairs. Each pair draws a grid for the game with three horizontal rows and three vertical rows, giving nine squares.

The aim is to make a line of three, which can be horizontal, diagonal or vertical.

Demonstrate the game on the board first with two students. The players first decide who is a nought – 0 – and who is a cross – X. In order to place a nought or a cross in the grid, players need to name some vocabulary or answer a question/form a sentence etc. correctly. For example, hold up a picture for the student to name. If he or she is correct, he or she places a nought or cross anywhere on the grid. The aim is to stop the other student from forming a line of three. Continue playing until one of the players manages to form a line of three noughts or three crosses. To use more language, students can make up a sentence or question containing the word and drill a specific question or sentence form.

|   |   |   |
|---|---|---|
| 0 | X |   |
| 0 | 0 |   |
| X | X | 0 |

|   |   |   |
|---|---|---|
|   | 0 |   |
| X | X | X |
|   |   |   |

|   |   |   |
|---|---|---|
| X | 0 | X |
| 0 | 0 | X |
| X |   | X |

**Odd One Out**

| Category | Step 5 speaking fluency and general language |
|---|---|
| Group size | Any/whole class |
| Level | Any |
| Materials | None |
| Preparation | You may want to prepare sets of five words if you cannot think off the cuff |

Write five words on the board. Students choose the 'odd one out', but they have to give you a valid reason *why*. An easy example:

white  green  apple  blue  brown

The most obvious answer is that an apple is a fruit, whereas the others are colours, or possibly that apple is a noun and the others are adjectives (beginners will not yet know that green can be a noun!). However, they could also say apple is the only word with the vowel a in it, or that starts with a vowel, that blue is the only word with four letters – the others all have five – or that only brown has just one vowel while the other words have two. Often, there are many possible answers.

Here is a grammar example:

cooked  flew  bought  saw  made

Here, cooked is the odd one out because it is the only regular verb. A pronunciation example could be:

toasted  cooked  wanted  painted  heated

Cooked is the odd one out because the 'ed' is pronounced 't' rather than 'id'.

Grammar:

church  dress  box  wish  woman

Woman is the odd one out because to make it plural you change an internal letter; all the others require -es. Or, wish is the only non-concrete noun. As long as someone can give you a valid reason for one term being 'odd', an answer is correct.

Students often enjoy compiling lists for other teams too. Be sure to give them a specific focus for each odd-one-out list.

**Old Maid**

| Category | Step 2 speaking drill |
|---|---|
| Group size | Divide into small groups of 4 to 6 students |
| Level | Beginner to intermediate |
| Materials | Pairs of cards, either pictures or words |
| Preparation | None |

Old Maid is a traditional card game where the aim is to avoid being the player left holding the 'old maid'. If playing with numbers, play with a regular card deck and extract three queens from the pack. Deal out the remaining cards. Players keep their cards to themselves and sort through them, taking out any pairs. Students must name the numbers in order to lay the pairs down on the table. The dealer then offers his or her hand – again, kept to him or herself – to the student on the left. This player takes a card and if it makes a pair with one of the cards in his or her hand then that pair can be placed down on the table and named. This second player then offers his or her hand to the next player, and so on, until one player is left holding the old maid, or queen.

**Language ideas**     To adapt this to diverse language possibilities, use sets of picture flashcards instead of playing cards. Specify the sentence or target structure to work on and whenever players have a pair of matching pictures they can lay them down and must say the designated sentence using the vocabulary shown in the pictures. For complete beginners, this may simply be naming the pictures, or making a short sentence dependent on the picture, such as 'I like apples.' You may want the students to use questions, in which case elicit 'Do you like apples?' A more complex question example is 'Did you buy any apples?' Adapt this game to your desired outcome and provide pictures or words that are suitable.

For intermediates, play with a selection of word cards. Students must make sentences using the word on the card. You could specify the tense the sentences should be in, or allow any type of sentence.

**Materials**     Each group of six students needs a set of picture cards. If you do not have anything suitable, put up a list of 12 words on the board and ask each adult to quickly sketch a pair of each. Provide blank playing card-sized cards for students to draw on. This allows you to have your materials made quickly and you can re-use the cards for many other games. Alternatively, use word cards.

**Pairs**

| | |
|---|---|
| Category | Reading and speaking drill |
| Group size | Any |
| Level | Beginner to advanced |
| Materials | Prepare sentences beforehand on paper, chop in two and shuffle |
| Preparation | Prepare the sentences you will use |

Write out some sentences you would like to work with. Chop them in two, then shuffle and distribute the halves to students. Give students a minute to remember the words on their paper. Allow a time limit for students to circulate and find their pair through repeating the line – there's to be no reading or showing the paper to other students. Use the same idea for proverbs, metaphors, riddles, jokes, expressions, or lines of poetry or songs.

**Parts of Speech Path Finder**

| Category | Step 2 grammar drill or fluency speaking |
|---|---|
| Group size | Divide into small groups of 4 students |
| Level | All levels |
| Materials | Print samples provided in the Appendix and fill in as required |
| Preparation | Quick if using template provided in Appendix |

This game can be used as a grammar drill for specific sentence types or tenses and as a fluency game for general language. Use the board game provided in the Appendix. You may want to enlarge it with a photocopier, stick it on cardboard and decorate it.

**Materials** You need a game board with at least 25 or 30 spaces, each space coloured in one of 4 or 5 colours. Four spaces have 'traps' (name these after grammatical errors) and three 'jump spots' (name these after, for example, famous novels).
You will also need:

- cards with the colours on them, as well as four trap cards and three jump ahead cards
- four to six game pieces to move per board
- a sheet providing the key for which colour stands for which part of speech

By using a key it's easy to change which parts of speech you use in a game. You could concentrate on prepositions of place, prepositions of time, adjectives, nouns, etc.

**Preparation** Decide what parts of speech you want to work on and match each one to a colour. For example, verbs = red, prepositions = yellow, etc. Draw the board and make the cards, if necessary. Use buttons for the game pieces.

**How to play** The first player draws a card and moves to the next space of that colour. The player checks the colour of the card against the key, and sees what part of speech it represents.

To stay on this spot, the player must give a word that matches the part of speech, and then use it in a sentence. (The next player can throw the die, move and pick up his or her card while the previous player is thinking up his or her sentence. This keeps the game moving along.) Set a time limit for a sentence to be produced, and, if incorrect, or not done in time, the player goes back two squares, or back to where he or she was at the start of that turn. It is sometimes an idea to put players in pairs for this game.

Players who draw a 'trap' card must go to that trap and lose a turn; players who draw a 'jump' card must go to the nearest jump spot. They don't lose a turn, but this move could send them backwards.

To win the game, the player must land on the last space and then give a sentence using all the parts of speech drilled in the game. If playing with beginners, skip this step, or simplify the requirement for the final square.

## Peer Editing

| Category | Reading and editing |
|---|---|
| Level | Beginner to advanced – good for mixed abilities |
| Group size | Any |
| Materials | None |
| Preparation | None |

Similarly to Buddy Reading, Peer Editing allows students to look at each other's work and make corrections and comments at their own levels. Pre-writing and rough drafts can be done independently. Advanced ESL students can be encouraged to write more, and with greater grammatical complexity. Peer editing is carried out as a last step before writing a final draft. Students can be encouraged to discuss content as well as grammar and punctuation.

## Personalization

| Category | Writing and speaking drill |
|---|---|
| Level | Beginner to intermediate |
| Group size | Any |
| Materials | None |
| Preparation | None |

When teaching a new grammatical structure it is useful to allow students to use this language to say something about themselves. So, for example, if

Shelley Ann Vernon

you are teaching conditionals, let students write three sentences about themselves using this, such as 'If I won the lottery I would ...' 'If I could take up a new hobby I would ...' 'If I could be anywhere in the world right now I would be ...'

Either provide three set sentences and allow students to complete them or let students make up their own sentences entirely. Students write these on paper, hand them to you, and you shuffle and re-distribute to the class. Everyone now guesses who said what by walking around and asking questions.

## Persuasion

| Category | Step 5 speaking fluency |
|---|---|
| Level | Intermediate to advanced |
| Group size | Any |
| Materials | Optional fact sheets |
| Preparation | Have students prepare for the game for homework using your chosen topic |

In pairs, students try to persuade other students to buy a product, vote for them, or take their point of view on a given topic. This sounds simple; however, you may find students do not have much to say and the conversation is forced or fizzles out. If you give a reason for the students to speak and to listen, you will find the conversation flows more readily.

For example, if you tell students to discuss their dream home, you may find that many students do not have much to say and are not too motivated. The activity is likely to come to an end very soon. The persuasion technique can be used to generate a reason to communicate and stimulate the students, and any topic can be discussed. It is as ideal for specialist subjects as it is for general language.

Here is a detailed example using the topic of dream homes. First, brainstorm with the class about ideal features for a dream home. With lower intermediates, jot down new vocabulary the class comes up with as they call out their ideas. Specify the type of information that is needed, such as location, proximity to services, environment, size, grounds, extra features such as pool or gym, parking, architectural style, whether modern or characterful, and so on. Now either give out real estate information on several homes to half of the students who are estate agents, or let students prepare descriptions of their ideal home for homework.

Once you have your dream home specifications, split the class into estate agents and homebuyers. Homebuyers have a few minutes to interview three or four estate agents and choose a property from those on offer. Estate agents only have one or two houses in their portfolio, which they are very keen to sell. House buyers may visit several estate agents with a time limit of a few minutes at each one before making their choice. See which estate agents make the most sales.

This is adaptable to many topics. Here are a few examples:

- favourite holiday destination: travel agents and customers
- best product: salespeople and customers
- favourite day out: tour guides and customers
- food to be served in school canteen: nutritionists and parents
- which school for your child: headmasters and parents
- which job: employers and job seekers
- which design: architects and buyers
- managers seeking to promote an employee
- which bank: bank managers and customers (ideal for business English). Give the bank managers the task of choosing a bank and reading up on the types of loans, rates and terms available for homework. The other students can prepare in a similar way with mortgages. In class see which bank managers recruit the most clients and which mortgage brokers make the most sales
- Which party: hosts describe what their party will be like and guests decide which party they want to go to
- Which political party: party leaders describe their policies and voters decide whom to vote for. Allow for some outrageous parties, such as the Monster Raving Loony Party in the UK. Be sure students know they can take on a role rather than express personal views. Have students each prepare a party manifesto for homework that can be used in the pair work in class
- Which city tour: tour guides try to recruit sightseers for their favourite city
- Which country? Ambassadors try to attract immigrants to their country. If you have refugees or feel that this is too sensitive a topic, play with imaginary countries that have fantasy ideas such as free food for children and so on
- Which pet: a pet lover tries to sell his or her idea of the best pet to a potential pet buyer

***Red pen/blue pen persuasion idea*** *Another teacher gave me the greater part of this idea. Half the students write down an item they think is useful and give it a realistic price value using a red pen. The others write down an item they think is useless and give it a reasonable price using a blue pen. All students fold papers, stand up and mill around – everyone must swap their paper three times in the space of one minute!*

*The students with items in red each have an item they must sell, and they must get as much as possible for the item because they desperately need the money. The other half have a fake item they are trying to sell to get money, but it's worthless.*

*Start the clock. Students have the obligation to sell an item and buy one before the time stops – tell them they have about five minutes, but you are not saying exactly when the time will run out. Students go around talking to the others to see what they have, how much it is and whether they want it. The idea is not to get stuck with an item in blue when the time is up. Anyone who has neither sold nor bought an item when time is up is also a loser, as if they had a blue item.*

## Picture Flashcards

| | |
|---|---|
| Category | Step 2 speaking drill |
| Group size | Small groups to large classes |
| Level | Beginner to lower intermediate |
| Materials | Pictures |
| Preparation | None |

Have the class or group sit in a circle if possible and pass a picture around. This could be a picture of a nurse, in which case each player takes the picture and says 'She's a nurse.' Once the first picture has got to the fourth student, add in a second picture, for example, 'He's a diver.' Each picture makes a complete circuit of the group with everyone saying the required sentence, or just the word. If students do not know the word they can ask someone next to them for help, but they cannot pass the picture on until they have named it out loud.

If you are in a traditional classroom setup the students can remain at their desks and pass the pictures to each other up and down the aisles. Keep handing out pictures until many pictures are circulating simultaneously.

At various points during the game blow a whistle or give a signal and all those holding pictures must do a group forfeit, if this is not too silly for your group of course. See under Forfeits for ideas.

## Picture Inspiration

| | |
|---|---|
| Category | Step 5 fluency |
| Level | Beginner to intermediate |
| Group size | Divide into small groups |
| Materials | None |
| Preparation | Have some suitable pictures to use if students do not bring any in and there are none in your textbook to use |

Ask a student to bring in a picture that he or she knows something about, preferably something interesting, such as a scene from a historical event, or something from a newspaper. For beginners, a photograph of a family member is appropriate, so students can work with more basic questions such as 'What is her name?' 'How old is she?' and so on. A holiday photograph is good for studying the past simple and past continuous: 'Where did you go?' 'What did you see?' 'What were you doing?'

Groups of students look at a picture and come up with a selection of questions about it. Allow a minute or two for students to write down their questions and then let them ask these to the person who brought in the picture. Use one picture per group of ten students maximum. If you have several groups, listen in to each one and note any recurring errors to go over afterwards.

### *Variation*

Bring in pictures of people from magazines and write a list of questions on the board to stimulate the students' imaginations. Give out one picture per student or pair of students and give them five or ten minutes to come up with a story about the person in the picture. With a small group, listen to all the stories, but with a large group just let the students tell one or two others their story. Questions you might choose are:

- What is this person's name?
- What does he look like?
- What does he do?
- What hobbies does he have?
- Does he have a girlfriend?
- Is he happy?

- Does he enjoy life?
- What secrets does he have?
- Does he have any pets?
- What is his daily life like?
- What is his ambition?
- What is he doing now?
- What will he be doing in five years' time?

## Poetry

| | |
|---|---|
| Category | Reading and Step 6 creative writing |
| Group size | Any |
| Level | Advanced |
| Materials | Poems |
| Preparation | Choose poems, or have students do so |

A challenging activity for advanced students is to translate a poem into English and then work in groups to improve the translation. If all your students share the same first language or nationality, choose a poem in their mother tongue, but if you have mixed languages/nationalities work on an existing translation into English so everyone has the same starting point.

Take this touching Urdu poem by Abdul Hafeez from Pakistan as an example. Give it to your students and see what they can do with it. There are no right answers! Don't force students to adopt your perceived improvements, since poetry appreciation is personal.

The first version below is the original translation from Urdu by the author, and the second is a reworked version with 'improvements', making the English more natural. Rhythm can be important in a poem and correct grammar may be sacrificed for poetic purposes.

**Original translation**

If I were Looking glass.
O' never ever in my life,
I'd be slave of opportunism.
Not only before the king,
but also at the gallows
only and only truth I'd speak,
If I were Looking glass.

**Re-worked version**

If I were Looking glass,
O' never in my life,
A liar would I be.
Before the king,
Or at the gallows,
Only truth would I speak,
If I were Looking glass.

| | |
|---|---|
| But for being human | But being flesh, |
| I'm born to be shattered | I'm shattered |
| ceaselessly, dear. | ceaselessly, dear. |
| Sometimes by shocks, | Sometimes by shocks, |
| Sometimes by fatal pangs | Sometimes by pangs |
| | of parting |
| O' parting with beloved. | Of parting with my beloved. |
| If I were Looking glass, | If I were Looking glass, |
| Surely I'd be crashed into | I'd be smashed into tiny |
| tiny pieces by ruthless stone | pieces by ruthless stone. |
| But only once, dear, | But only once, dear, |
| it would happen to me in life. | Would it happen to me, |
| If I were Looking glass. | If I were Looking glass. |

## Population Punctuation

| | |
|---|---|
| Category | Step 3 reading and sentence construction |
| Group size | Group work |
| Level | Beginner to advanced (excellent for grammar) |
| Materials | Words written out on pieces of paper |
| Preparation | Decide on the sentences you will work with |

This game is excellent for general language and also for focusing on a particular grammatical structure. Write out sentences using one card or piece of paper per word. Include cards/papers for punctuation marks, such as commas and full stops. With the students in groups, or with the whole of a small class, give each student but one a card. The one without arranges the other students so as to form a correct sentence. This game suits students who learn kinaesthetically. Movement also helps keep your students from dropping off during your class!

You could play to see who can make the longest correct sentence in a given time limit, or give two groups the same sentence and have them race against each other to make up a correct sentence using all the words and punctuation.

This is a good game to play to work on apostrophes, especially if you give out word cards and apostrophes separately. You could also separate elements such as irregular plural endings, for example in 'They went to the children's playground.'

For sentences such as 'It's a long way to the Sahara' and 'Have the custard on its own' you could say the sentence out loud; then students need to make up the sentence with the elements they have and decide whether or not an apostrophe is needed. Many English native speakers are confused about use of the apostrophe, so time spent on it will not be wasted!

## Presentation

| | |
|---|---|
| Category | Step 5 speaking fluency |
| Group size | Any |
| Level | Lower intermediate to advanced |
| Materials | None |
| Preparation | Students prepare this for homework |

Students each need to prepare a presentation on a given topic for homework. For best results, allow them to choose their own topics. For intermediates, three minutes is long enough, but you could go up to ten minutes or more with advanced learners. If you have a small group presentations can be longer, but with a large class you will have to keep them short or you will not have time to listen to everyone's during the course of a series of lessons. Tell students they cannot read out their presentation, but must do it from memory, using only bullet-pointed notes. This means students will have to rehearse delivering their talks in advance in order to achieve a degree of fluency and confidence.

When commenting on presentations after delivery, it is best to point out the things that the student handled well. Have other students comment on what they liked. This is better than picking the presentation apart, which is discouraging, and can make the other students nervous about delivering their own presentations.

Pointers for giving good presentations are:

- know your topic well
- tell the audience what you are going to tell them, then tell them, and then tell them what you told them – i.e. have an introduction, main content and summary
- vary your tone and speed of speech
- make eye contact with the audience and seem confident
- speak clearly and at the beginning check the audience can hear you
- use an anecdote, story or metaphor to illustrate a point
- keep any visuals simple and colourful
- rehearse repeatedly in sections until you are confident

Giving presentations is popular with business English students, especially if the topics are business related.

## Present Perfect

| | |
|---|---|
| Category | Step 2 speaking drill – fluency element possible |
| Group size | Class work in small groups |
| Level | Beginner to lower intermediate |
| Materials | None |
| Preparation | Decide what the 'Have you ever ...' questions will be |

This game practises the present perfect and past tense, particularly questions. Demonstrate first by bringing one student up to the front. The student has to answer 'Yes' to the first question but after that can answer whatever he or she likes. You ask the student a question such as 'Have you ever eaten tiramisu?' The student has to answer yes whether he or she has eaten it or not. Ask three more questions such as: 'What are the ingredients?' 'Where did you eat the tiramisu?' 'Did you like it?' Have a limit of three or four questions and let the class decide whether the student has in fact eaten tiramisu or not.

Now split the class into groups and let them play the game with a series of questions of their own. If your students cannot think of any questions, you will need to write some ideas on the board, such as 'Have you ever been to Japan?' 'Have you ever ridden a horse?' and so on. It is better if students can think of their own questions and thus use the 'Have you ever ...' structure from memory rather than just reading from the board, although you could, of course, omit this phrase from your board cues.

## Problem Solving

| | |
|---|---|
| Category | Step 5 speaking fluency |
| Group size | All sizes |
| Level | Intermediate to advanced |
| Materials | None |
| Preparation | Decide on the problems students to discuss |

Give students a problem to solve and let them discuss how to go about it in small groups. Then let a member from each group present the solution to the class and see what the different solutions are. For problems to use, ask your students for ideas, and look in the media for current issues. There is no shortage of problems, which can be focused on any area of vocabulary that you want to study. Examples are: 'There is too much traffic at rush hour.' 'Graffiti is a problem.' 'Cheap housing can be depressing,' and so on.

## Punctuation

| Category | Step 3 reading for punctuation |
|---|---|
| Level | Intermediate to advanced |
| Group size | Any |
| Materials | None |
| Preparation | Take a reading passage, remove all punctuation and give this to the students |

Provide sentences or paragraphs without punctuation. Let the students punctuate the sentences, but see if they can think of different versions of the same sentence where the meaning changes because of the punctuation. For example:

- 'A woman without her man is nothing.' / 'A woman: without her, man is nothing.'
- 'A panda eats shoots and leaves.' / 'A panda eats, shoots and leaves.' (See Lynne Truss's excellent book on pronunciation.)

The words 'Run Paul Samuel said no' without punctuation give rise to various possibilities:

- 'Run,' Paul Samuel said. 'No!'
- 'Run, Paul! Samuel said no!'
- 'Run!' Paul Samuel said 'No.'

See also the longer tongue twisters that would be fun to punctuate.

Ask students to punctuate sentences, such as:

- The judges decision is final. / The judge's decision is final.
- The childrens playgrounds over there. / The            children's playground's over there.
- Those peoples children did it. / Those people's children did it.
- The womens clothes are on this floor. / The women's clothes are on this floor.

See also the game Population Punctuation.

**Pyramid**

| | |
|---|---|
| Category | Speaking vocabulary revision or grammar drill |
| Group size | Any, divided into two teams |
| Level | Flexible |
| Materials | 20 index cards, ten pieces of construction paper, markers |
| Preparation | Come up with a minimum of 30 different topics that could head a category and at least 10 words that fit each one to be sure that there are enough possible clues |

This activity can either be a quick game or a vocabulary-building project over a couple of classes, depending on how you want to handle the preparation. It can be used for speaking fluency and vocabulary in variation 1 and as a grammar drill in variation 2.

In the lesson before the game, break the students into two groups and have each of them think up ten lists.

**How to play**     Divide the class into two teams. Each team has ten cards with different categories on them made by the other team. Assign each category a certain number of points. Make harder ones worth more.

Hand the first person on one team a card. This person turns to the next player on the team and tries to give clues about the category. The category cannot be read out loud. The player with the card has to think of things that belong on the list to say as clues.

The pair has 30 seconds for the second player to guess the category. If they succeed, the player that guessed gets the next card, and turns to the third member of the team to give clues. This goes on until someone fails to guess the category in the 30-second time limit. Then play switches to the next team.

An example round might be:

Player 1: Poppy, dandelion, rose …

Player 2: Flowers!

Player 1: Yes!

If you had the students make the categories up, it is important to make sure that the teams don't work with the categories they made up themselves.

The team that gets through all their cards first gets to go to the challenge round. In this, the winning team picks its best two players to get to the top of the pyramid in two to three minutes (depending on the level of play). The pyramid is set up with the construction paper stuck to the board in a pyramid shape: one on top, two on the next level, three on the next, and four squares of paper across the bottom. The easier categories are on the bottom, and they get more challenging as the players progress. The player that will guess sits with his or her back to the pyramid. The one to give clues sits facing the pyramid so that he or she can see each card as it is turned over. When one card is guessed, the next in the pyramid is turned over. If all the categories are guessed in the allotted time, award bonus points as well. It's a good idea to have some kind of prize for the pyramid round.

For a harder variation, students can guess the specific word within the category.

### Variation

Instead of categories with lists, make up quiz questions about whatever information or grammar you want to drill. Use the time limit to get students to answer or pass as quickly as possible. Since they won't be guessing categories, they won't need as much time to answer, so cut it to 30 seconds for the regular round and one minute for the Challenge round.

To play with beginners, make simple questions such as 'What is your name?' 'Where do you live?' and so on. To drill grammar, the student with the card asks 'Where are you going at the weekend?' and the student answering must give any grammatically correct reply that fits the question. The challenge is to answer correctly within the timeframe and to make it to the final round.

GAMES Q–R

**Qualities**

| Category | Step 5 speaking fluency |
|---|---|
| Group size | Any size |
| Level | Intermediate to advanced |
| Materials | None |
| Preparation | Think of a diverse range of jobs, or ask students in class. Ask students to prepare a paragraph on the qualities needed for a certain job, possibly for homework. Collect these and use them for the activity |

This speaking activity deals with personal qualities, talents, skills, strengths and weaknesses. Take a list of jobs such as sales manager, typist, conservationist, shop owner, physical education teacher, university professor, banker, stockbroker and part-time help at a school canteen. You may want to use some of the jobs your students have to personalize the activity, but make the jobs varied, and including indoor and outdoor, physical and cerebral, social and solitary. You need half as many jobs as you have students, so if you have 30 students you need 15 different jobs. Students, in pairs, come up with a list of qualities needed to perform one of these jobs well, and another of the qualities or personal attributes that would be a problem. Have students write their lists on two cards, one for pros and one for cons.

Now seat the students in two rows, facing each other. The pairs that worked together to create the cards should be split up. Each student holds a job attribute card: those on one side are employers and those opposite are candidates or employees. The candidate has the qualities described on his or her card; the employer has to find a suitable candidate for the job on his or her card. NB employers and candidates do not tell each other what the job on their respective cards is – they just interview each other and see if there is a match. Give a time limit for the interviews and once this is up let candidates move along one seat so all the employers get to interview all the candidates, or allow a set amount of interviews, after which employers must make a selection from those interviewed.

There are umpteen ways in which to vary this idea. For example:

- Give out job cards in advance and conduct role-play interviews according to what is on the cards.
- Let students describe what they are good at and like doing and what their weaknesses are, and let other students suggest jobs to them as a careers guidance role-play.
- Students think of a job, describe the attributes needed for that job and let the other students guess what it is. This can be done in teams with a time limit for guessing the job and points awarded to the teams for correct guesses.
- Students interview other students and choose someone in class to take over their current job.

## Questionnaires

| | |
|---|---|
| Category | Step 5 speaking fluency |
| Group size | Any size |
| Level | Beginner to advanced |
| Materials | Questionnaires |
| Preparation | Have the students prepare questionnaires on a given topic for homework, or as the teacher do this beforehand |

This is a useful speaking activity that gets the students out of their seats and moving around. Design a questionnaire and let students interview each other for answers. For beginners, questionnaires can involve questions such as place of birth, home address, number of children, pets, likes and dislikes. For more advanced students, you may venture into any topics such as finding out people's views on current events. For example, in France, at the time of writing, there had recently been a spate of attacks by dogs on children, which was being reported in the media. A questionnaire could aim to find out how many in the class own dogs and how many have been known to bite, or whether the students know of any people who have been bitten, how badly injured they were, and views on various measures that could be taken. With advanced students, let the students come up with a list of questions for the questionnaire themselves and then circulate in class to gather opinions.

## *Variation*

For a variation, allow students to write their own questions that they would like to ask others. This will give them more motivation. As students are writing their questions, go around the class and make they are accurate. If you cannot get around to everyone, then just do your best! Pair a weaker student up with a stronger one so that the former learns from the latter.

## Quizzes

| | |
|---|---|
| Category | Writing questions and Step 5 speaking fluency |
| Group size | All group sizes |
| Level | High beginner to advanced |
| Materials | Questions, which can be prepared for homework |
| Preparation | The class prepares questions for homework |

Ask the class for a topic that interests them – pop music, sport, general knowledge, history – and tell them to prepare a quiz, say five questions and answers each, for homework. You could receive and mark/check the questions in advance, or not, as you prefer, although the benefit of marking the questions first is that this may help students formulate questions correctly during the class.

During the lesson, divide students into small teams. You, or a student, hold all the questions and ask each team in turn a question from the list, awarding points for correct answers and triple points for correct answers given using correct grammar. A star student can be given the job of deciding if questions are accurate and thus awarding single or triple points. Being given a responsible role should keep a more advanced student challenged; otherwise, he or she may become bored.

For a quiz to work well, it is crucial that the questions are interesting to your students, regardless of whether they are to you. With teens, for example, I did a 'guess who'-style quiz about a pop icon I knew they liked, and they were chuffed (pleased!) when they guessed the answer – the person in question meant something to them, whereas a political figure may have received a very different reaction.

A grand quiz can be prepared over part of several lessons; for example, 15 minutes at the end of a number of lessons could be spent working on quiz questions, in order to add some variety. Students could work in small groups or individually. Providing themes may help focus their minds, but do leave students to come up with and write their own questions.

Questions can be hard to come up with and trickier to write than stating facts. Therefore have students write one fact on a piece of paper, for example, 'The capital city of Scotland is Edinburgh.' Students swap papers and write the question form of the statement, in this case 'What is the capital city of Scotland?' 'Who is the President of the USA?' 'Where is Sydney?' and so on. Repeat this process a few times, as, in addition to drilling questions, if the same questions are used in a quiz the class has a better chance of getting answers right. To help, have question words written on the board as prompts: when, what, where, why, how, who, which.

If you have any students who are way ahead of all the others, send them around to check the grammar of questions being prepared. You should collect and mark all the questions so that correct grammar is reinforced during quiz time.

*In order to involve more students during a quiz and avoid them sitting passively, waiting for a turn, ask a question to Team A. All team members then write their answers pieces of paper and pass these to members of team B – make this logical according to your classroom setup so as not to waste lots of time passing papers. Reveal the answer, then correct answers are passed to a collection point. Discard incorrect answers. Then swap over. This will ensure that every single student listens to the questions – with everyone either writing or reading an answer, the whole class is actively involved.*

*At the end of the game, count up how many correct answers you have for each team to see who wins.*

For an immediate quiz with no preparation, students could turn sentences into questions, change the tense of a sentence or question, provide a synonym for a word or describe the meaning of a word.

**Quiz Race**

| | |
|---|---|
| Category | Reading and writing |
| Group size | All group sizes |
| Level | Beginner to advanced |
| Materials | Reading passage with questions prepared in advance |

| Preparation | Choose your reading passage and write the questions or use this idea with passages in your textbook if you have one |
| --- | --- |

Explain the purpose of the activity, which is to improve general language skills and vocabulary through reading and to see how quickly students can scan written material for information.

Give the students a text to read and make sure the topic is of interest to them. This could be something from a magazine, the paper, song lyrics, a poem, an extract from a play, or a passage from the textbook you are using, if you have one. Start writing up questions about the passage on the board. As soon as you start writing, students race to answer your questions by scanning the written material. Your first questions may not concern the first paragraph, but could relate to information given in the middle of the passage. Students can write their answers in note form or as full sentences, as you wish. When you have finished writing out the last question, allow another 30 seconds and stop the activity. Students see how many questions they have answered. Repeat this with a different passage. Students are sure to be quicker the second time around.

As an additional option, once students have completed this activity, you may like to ask them to think of an additional question about the passage, which they ask a class member.

*The trick to this traditional reading comprehension activity is to give a tight time limit to add an element of excitement, and to use topics that the students are interested in.*

## Radio Broadcasts And Transcriptions

| Category | Listening fluency and speaking fluency variant |
| --- | --- |
| Group Size | Any |
| Level | Intermediate and upwards |
| Materials | A listening resource free online. BBC radio is available free online and is perfect for British accents. CNN is a renowned source of news in America |
| Preparation | Finding a suitable resource |

### *Listening for information*

Let students listen to an online broadcast for homework and prepare questions for their fellow classmates. In the next lesson, students team up and quiz other teams using the questions they prepared for homework. The winners are both the team with the most correct answers and the team with the most unanswered questions.

### Listen and deliver a summary

Another way to use radio is to have students listen to a variety of broadcasts and prepare a summary of one of them. In the next lesson students should present the information they have heard and try to make it sound as fascinating as possible. Having listened to a handful of presentations, the class votes as to which broadcast they would like to hear in full.

This is a good multi-level activity: the stronger students could prepare the presentations while the others listen.

### Use broadcasts and their transcriptions for listening

Use radio shows or broadcasts and their transcriptions for a fill-in-the-blanks listening activity. Give students a homework task to source a broadcast and its transcription online. On CNN (at the time of writing) you will find a link to a transcription just below a news item. Copy and paste this transcription into a document and delete words. Whatever words you delete will be points of focus, therefore delete those to which you would like to draw attention, such as grammar or specific vocabulary. Students could record themselves reading the transcription and bring this into class, or, if you have a reliable internet connection in your classroom, use the original broadcast. However, the task of recording the transcription is excellent for speaking fluency.

### Reader's Theatre

| Category | Speaking and reading fluency |
|---|---|
| Group Size | Any |
| Level | Flexible |
| Materials | A fiction story full of dialogue that can be converted into a play, or an actual play/text converted in advance. Be sure that the story has an appropriate number of parts for each group; two colours of highlighters or some other way to mark the text |

| Preparation | You may need to convert a story into a play ahead of this task |
|---|---|

This is a co-operative activity for the entire class. The main objective here is to increase fluency and expression in reading aloud. Along with this, materials can be chosen to focus on certain content area objectives, vocabulary or grammar points.

Pre-teach any important vocabulary, then hand out the fiction text to students. Read the text aloud to students and have them highlight any dialogue. (This is an excellent opportunity to review quotation marks!)

Then have the students exchange papers and compare them in pairs. They should check to see if they and their partners have highlighted correctly.

Read the story together as a class and mark the key sentence in the narrative with the second highlighter colour. Make these lines the narrator's part. Discuss why a narrator is important.

You have two choices at this point. Have students take parts and read the highlighted text as if it were a script, or collect the papers, prepare a typed script from the highlighted version and perform the play in the next class.

This activity can run for 45–90 minutes, depending on how much of the text preparation you do in class.

**Play performance**
- hand out scripts and assign the roles in the play
- read the text chorally if you feel students need it
- perform the play as a class
- if possible, tape the performance to listen to later
- if there is room, have students get up and perform the play, with some basic staging

**Reading Comprehension**

| Category | Reading |
|---|---|
| Group Size | Any |
| Level | Flexible |
| Materials | Text from textbook, online, books, magazines, articles, papers or student written material |
| Preparation | Finding a suitable text |

Rather than give students a text with questions, let them write the questions for their classmates. This involves students more actively in the task rather than them simply scanning for often rather obvious answers.

A way to spice up this activity is to give a time limit for the task. For example, students prepare 10 questions for homework and bring these into class. Half the students have prepared questions for reading passage A; the others have done passage B. In class, students swap reading passages and each has a time limit to answer the set of questions given by their partner.

In a mixed-ability class, put strong pupils together; if they finish early they can go around the room checking grammar or helping other students with their answers.

### *Variation*

A fun variation is to let students read the passage they have been given once, and then try to answer as many questions as possible from the list without referring to the passage again. These initial answers are worth five points each, if correct. The student then gets a second reading and a second chance at any questions he or she could not answer the first time around. These answers, if correct, earn three points each. Then add up the score and swap over. This could be done as pair work, or in teams, with a panel of students working together and the most advanced student chairing the quiz.

## Reading Treasure Hunt

| | |
|---|---|
| Category | Step 3 reading – scanning for grammar and vocabulary |
| Group size | Any |
| Level | Beginner to intermediate |
| Materials | A reading passage |
| Preparation | Decide what your students will look for in the passage |

Students are given a reading passage and use coloured pencils to highlight certain words or grammatical structures that you specify. For example, you might ask students to read the passage and underline any irregular verb forms in orange and any prepositions in blue. Or students can hunt through looking for any question or statement in a given tense, and so on. You might ask students to search for a collection of vocabulary words for which you give clues. Alternatively, to avoid spending preparation time yourself, ask students to work in pairs or small groups and come up with a list of 10 words with clues for students from another group to find. Allow dictionaries for this, or allow a limited use of the dictionary, for example, students may look up three words only when solving their colleagues' clues. Beginners can perform simple tasks such as finding certain given words, or underlining verbs, prepositions or conjunctions and so on. Let students compare answers with each other as a variation to including the whole class.

## Relay Race And Advanced Variant

| Category | Step 2 speaking drill |
|---|---|
| Group size | Any |
| Level | Beginner to intermediate |
| Materials | None |
| Preparation | None |

**How to play**   Put your group into teams of approximately five players and ask them to line up behind each other. The player at the front has a picture of, say, a pizza. On your signal, the first player in each line says to the second, 'Would you like some pizza?' He or she says 'Yes please,' takes the picture, turns to the third person, and asks 'Would you like some pizza?' and so on, until you reach the end of the line. The idea is to get the pizza down to the end of the line as quickly as possible. If you have a longer line of ten people, for example, then you should pass down at least two different pictures, one after the other, to keep everyone involved.

Once all the pictures are at the bottom of the line, the person at the end of the line runs up to the front with them.

It is most important that the words are properly pronounced and that accuracy is not abandoned for speed. To ensure this, have referees, perhaps the first person in each line, monitor each team. Swap the referees around, but make sure the students chosen are up to the task.

**Language ideas**   Use any language you like for this game, from simply naming the item and passing it down to speaking longer sentences with a particular verb tense or structure. Drill ideas for beginners are, for example, 'I am Rosa [turning to the person behind her] and you are Amin.' Amin continues with 'I am Amin and you are Mikhail,' and so on.

This could continue:

Rosa: 'I love ice-cream.'

Amin: 'I love chocolate.'
Mikhail: 'I love coffee.'

Rosa: 'I love ice-cream.'
Amin: 'She loves ice-cream and I love chocolate.'
Mikhail: 'She loves chocolate, I love coffee,' etc.

Rosa: 'I like ice-cream. What do you like?'
Amin: 'I like chocolate. What do you like?'
Mikhail: 'I like cake ...'

This game can even be useful for advanced players if you would like to drill an aspect of language where they frequently make errors.

You do not have to use a picture, but can just pass a message or a word – written or not – down the line.

### *Variation*

For intermediate to advanced students, use the Relay Race variation. Instead of handing down vocabulary cards or having set sentences repeated down the line of students, give your pupils the more challenging task of coming up with their own sentences during the race. For example, hand a picture card to the first student in each team, and this student has to make up a sentence about that picture. The student then passes the card to the next person in the team and this person has to make up a different sentence, and so on.

Instead of a picture, hand or say a word to the first student. This student makes up a sentence or a question containing that word. This allows intermediate students to use a much wider range of language. If you use this exercise as a fluency game, then you would not focus on correcting the language at all during the activity. You might note a few errors and go over them on the board afterwards.

### Remember And Write

| Category | Spelling and vocabulary revision |
|---|---|
| Group size | Any |
| Level | Beginner to lower intermediate |
| Materials | Pictures, objects or words |
| Preparation | None |

Display at least 12 picture cards on the board. Give the class a limited time to look at and remember all the items; then cover them and allow a couple of minutes for students to write down as many items as they remember. Use pictures for vocabulary retention and words for spelling.

I used to enjoy playing this game as a child, using a tray with 12 objects on. We had to remember them before the tray was covered by a tea towel. Using real objects adds a fun element, but all activities that force us to think are enjoyable.

## Re-Order It

| | |
|---|---|
| Category | Step 3 reading |
| Level | Beginner to advanced |
| Group size | Divide students into small groups |
| Materials | Text on pieces of paper |
| Preparation | Cut up a passage of text |

Take an interesting text such as a poem, a story, an article, or lines from a play, great novel or work of literature. Use any written material that is best adapted to the level of your group. A nursery rhyme or children's story might be suitable for beginners, while a Shakespearean sonnet may be suitable for very advanced students (bearing in mind that these are a challenge even for native speakers!).

Cut up the text into portions and give these out to small groups of students. Each student has a minimum of one portion of text. You can use different texts for the different groups or give each group the same text.

Now, using a time limit to increase the students' focus, let the groups work out the correct order of the text. Each student reads (aloud if this suits) his or her text and, speaking only in English, they order the pieces correctly.

## Rhyming Challenge

| | |
|---|---|
| Category | Step 2 speaking drill (can also be done as a writing game) |
| Group size | Divide into small groups |
| Level | Intermediate to advanced |
| Materials | None |
| Preparation | None aside from some examples for your demonstration |

Divide the class into approximately six students or fewer per team. Write six words per team on the board, or just write six words for all teams to work with. Allow two or three minutes for students to huddle together in a group and come up with a word that rhymes with each of the words on the board and a specified sentence type containing that word. Time this activity, and let students know when one minute has passed and when there are only 30 seconds left. This puts a little pressure on, adding an element of fun and increasing the focus. When the time is up, a student from team A reads out his or her rhyming words and sentences. Award a point for a correct rhyming word and three points for a correct sentence. Move swiftly round the teams, with each team member taking a turn to give a sentence. Do not stop to correct sentences mid-game, but take notes and write – or ask the students to write – the sentences with errors on the board at the end of the game, and let the class correct them. It should take a minute or two only to hear all the sentences and award the points, so keep the game moving.

As a variation, play with no writing. This forces students to think of and remember sentences.

For best use of this activity as a speaking drill, tell the students exactly what sentence formation you want them to create with the rhymes for the given words. Here is an example for lower intermediate students.

Target structure: simple past
Words: bought, ran, ate, pen, eat, walked

Example sentences
| | | |
|---|---|---|
| bought: taught | He taught English. |
| ran: pan | She cooked pasta in a pan. |
| ate: late | She was late for class. |
| pen: men | The men went to the same college. |
| eat: sweet | They ate lots of sweet food. |
| walked: talked | He talked to his brother yesterday. |

Here is another, difficult, example using the present perfect. Students need to make up sentences using the present perfect and containing a word that rhymes with the one given.

Target structure: present perfect
Words: cat, mean, beach, cold, ship, bread

144

Example sentences

| | |
|---|---|
| cat: flat | I have lived in a flat. |
| mean: seen | I have never seen the Eiffel Tower. |
| reach: beach | He has been to the beach today. |
| cold: told | They have told her to do her homework. |
| ship: trip | She has visited Germany on a school trip. |
| bread: read | Have you read any novels in English? |

*A tip for the students is first to brainstorm words that rhyme and then see which ones fit well into sentences using the target structure.*

**Rivet**

| | |
|---|---|
| Category | Vocabulary review, recognition and word shape |
| Group size | Any |
| Level | Beginner to intermediate |
| Materials | Class board and pens |
| Preparation | Select the vocabulary words you will play with |

Rivet focuses on vocabulary and word recognition using a list of related words taken from a reading or vocabulary list. It also involves structured teacher-to-student interaction with limited vocabulary, and both high- and low-level students can play the same game with the proper preparation. The actual prep for the game is minimal, but must be preceded by a lesson that includes the vocabulary that will be used. Alternatively, pick words that students already know from previous classes, as this game does not work with completely unfamiliar vocabulary. Choose three to five words that come under a related topic. They can be from a reading passage, or a lesson's vocabulary. Write the topic on the top of the board. Draw spaces on the board for each word, indicating the number of letters for each word.

**How to play**    Point out the topic to the students and discuss it briefly if necessary. Tell the students that the blanks on the board represent words related to the topic and that they are to guess them. Students will have three chances to guess the word before you give them a letter to help. The object of the game is to guess the words as quickly as possible. The students do not spell the words. If they guess a letter, then they are

145

probably confusing the game with Hangman. Remind the students that you will not take any letter guesses, only words.

The original version is a co-operative game, but this can also be played in teams. Give each word five points. For every wrong guess, take off one point. The team that guesses the word gets awarded however many points are attached to it at that moment. The team that has the most points at the end is the winner.

### Variation

Instead of blanks, draw a silhouette of the word, showing tall letters and those that hang below the line. This helps with recognizing words as a whole unit. Again, after three guesses, reveal a letter.

## Role-Plays

| Category | Speaking fluency or drill |
|---|---|
| Group Size | Work in small groups |
| Level | Flexible |
| Materials | Scripts which may be student written |
| Preparation | Choose or write the script or have students write it |

Role-plays are excellent speaking opportunities. For beginners, they can be highly structured, where students repeat a given dialogue such as going to the shop to buy some groceries. For intermediates and up, students have more language to make up dialogues as they go along. Role-plays are best done in pairs or small groups of up to six people. Too many students per group will limit speaking opportunities, and you are more likely to have one or two students dominate.

Role-plays help students relax and express themselves freely, as they are not responsible for what they say – it is the *character* speaking. Role-plays can also be very good for shy students, helping them come out of the woodwork as they hide behind a role.

Choose role-play topics that your students relate to, such as a job interview, parents and teenagers, sharing a house with friends, a neighbour with terrible habits, being a dissatisfied customer and so on. Take care to avoid any sensitive topic that may upset them. The best way to get good ideas for role-plays that interest your class is to ask them!

Offer guidance for the role-play as required. With beginners, this will mean demonstrating the role-play with a student, showing the written dialogue, or having students read this out or hear it several times on audio before you can expect them to perform it from memory. With intermediates and advanced students, give out roles to the students with guidelines as to what they should say or who they are in a given circumstance. For example, you could recreate a business meeting where one student is a boss who wants to fire someone, another is a person who is never prepared and who other workers feel is lazy, another cannot pay attention at the meeting and always interrupts, while another is thinking of quitting the company. Students receive a card with their character outline and proceed to play out the scene spontaneously. For intermediates, it's best if students get their personality specs and the main theme of the role-play in a previous lesson and prepare some lines or thoughts for homework. This will make the actual live role-play more fluid.

An interesting thing to do once the role-play has played itself out the first time is to swap the roles around by letting students draw them randomly. The second version will not necessarily be the same, given that students have new roles, plus an increased familiarity with the situation and language. It may well be better!

Once the students have the right idea, ask them for ideas about what role-plays to tackle. Your students will certainly come up with many interesting situations from their own lives. Ask them to make up character cards, which you can use in subsequent classes.

This idea can be used for a wide range of topics and it is especially useful if you are teaching English to adults for a particular profession, such as nursing or engineering. Here, role-plays can focus on work situations that your students are likely to find themselves in. Business English students often want to role-play staff or sales meetings. For general English, try topics like:

- Choosing the family holiday, with each family member having different preferences. The family have to reach a consensus or there is no holiday!
- One family member wanting to move to a different place for work, or to the country, while another wants to stay in the same place/the city.
- Debating what the group/family budget will be spent on: private school fees, an extension to the house, investment in a business or paying off the mortgage early.
- Government ministers arguing over their share of the pie: housing, agriculture, health, national security, police ...

- A school deciding how to spend a big grant. The students could take on roles of the different subject teachers wanting a new science lab, new gym, field trips, or to sponsor the best students. The head teacher chairs the meeting.
- Identify a real-life situation and ask students to prepare roles relating to it for homework. A newspaper article will usually set forth elements of the debate to help students furnish their role-play.

**Shopping role-play**    Make some students store keepers and give them each a list of the items they stock. Make the bulk of the students shoppers and give them a list of items each to buy – these lists can differ. Let the students have a time limit to go out and buy all the items they need. There may be one item on the lists that does not exist in the shops, so any student(s) with this list will not be able to complete the task. Those students could then become the shopkeepers in a second round.

**Easy prep role-play**    A variation on preparing for role-plays is to do something less structured, perhaps with fewer roles. Write a difficult situation on the board, such as two people arguing about why they missed a train and blaming each other, and where had been beforehand.

Now, split the students up, half being one character and half the other. Let them write down as many things that they can think of that their character would say. Then have a couple of students stand up – probably the more able – and demonstrate the argument.

Once everyone has seen the dialogue in action, let them pair up and try their own creative argument. Blow a whistle every minute (or more if you see that most people are still arguing) and all students swap partners.

**Round Robin**

| Category | Step 5 speaking fluency |
|---|---|
| Level | Beginner to intermediate |
| Group size | One or more with the class divided into small groups of up to eight students or so per group |
| Materials | A soft ball or some paper crunched into a ball and pencil and paper for the students |
| Preparation | None |

This is a great game for working on all kinds of small talk, so is good for speaking fluency. The example given here relates to advice, but you're not limited to this. There's also no out-of-class preparation, so you can play Round Robin at any time. You may, though, need 10 or 15 minutes' preparation in class depending on your students and the lesson you are teaching.

Each student needs to write down or keep in mind a mild complaint or problem, such as 'I'm cold' or 'I have a headache.' With low-level students, discuss these beforehand, and have students write down possible advice for such problems on another sheet of paper. For example, if a student is assigned the problem 'I'm cold,' then discuss responses such as 'I'll turn up the heating' or 'I'll close the window.' You may want to rehearse the short conversations chorally. More advanced students should be able to work without writing down the phrases.

Before you start the activity, ask students to think about ways of giving advice, and write phrases on the board, such as 'you should', 'why don't you', 'you ought to', 'if I were you I would', 'it would be best if you', 'you could try', 'you had better' and so on. With lower levels, give three to four options only. As the activity goes on, gradually remove these prompts so students are forced to speak from memory.

**How to play**    The teacher starts off by tossing a ball to a student, who states his or her problem: 'I'm cold.' The student throws the ball to someone else. The person who catches the ball responds to the complaint with simple advice like 'Would you like a jacket?' or 'I'll close the window.' The first student should respond appropriately with 'Thank you,' or 'Yes, please.' Now the student who has the ball states a complaint, throws the ball to someone else, and starts everything over.

This is a co-operative game, so there aren't any winners or losers. You could set a goal to see how quickly everyone completes one turn. This would encourage fluency.

It's best to keep this game light rather than get into real problems. Use fictional characters to avoid being personal and offending people. For example, avoid 'I am getting divorced.' Instead, use 'My friend is getting divorced.'

### *Variations*

Instead of discussing complaints, discuss personal history. This resembles a common type of small talk. Allow students to pretend to be someone else if they prefer (their own personal history may be too distressing to share). Of course, they don't have to tell the truth either – as long as the English they use is correct, it doesn't matter!

As a second option, use hobbies and activities. Students make comments about what they do in their free time: 'I like to read.' 'I play tennis on Wednesdays.' Again, this is based on a common type of small talk.

GAMES S

## Sentence Play Off

| | |
|---|---|
| Category | Step 5 speaking fluency or writing |
| Level | Intermediate to advanced |
| Group size | Any |
| Materials | None |
| Preparation | Prepare a few examples for a demonstration if you cannot think off the cuff |

See how many sentences your students can come up with that all contain a given word. For example, give a word such as 'paint'. It is good to choose a word that has more than one function, for example one that can be a verb or a noun. Allow two minutes for all the students – in groups or individually – to write down as many sentences as possible containing the word. You could then have a play off between teams, ping-pong style, and see which team has the most correct sentences. Examples include: 'I can paint.' 'Can you paint?' 'I love painting.' 'He paints every week.' 'I need some paint.' 'Please buy me some paint.' With advanced students, bypass the writing stage and play directly as a speaking game.

If using this as a writing idea, let all students choose a word, write it at the top of a piece of paper and add one sentence that contains it. Then pass the paper on to the next person, who adds a second sentence. Let the papers circulate around several students, each time adding a sentence of their own containing the specified word, until you have about five sentences on each. At the end, let students mark the paper they are holding, correcting any errors they spot in the sentences. Then students get together in small groups in order to attempt to eradicate all errors from the papers. The teacher circulates and tells students when they have finished, or if there is still an error to correct. When one group has finished, the group members can split up to join other groups and help them finish.

## Sequences

| | |
|---|---|
| Category | Step 3 reading/spelling drill |
| Level | All levels, but most productive for beginners |
| Group size | A pair-work game for any class size |
| Materials | Cards |
| Preparation | Examples and a blank are included with the printable appendix. The teacher may print these in advance or students make their own and cut them up in class |

Use this game to teach words in sequence, such as the days of the week or the months of the year, or a sequence of words in alphabetical order. The game is played in pairs with players facing each other.

If you are teaching the months of the year, you need 4 sets of 12 cards for every pair of players. Use the sheet provided in the Appendix that is included with this book as a download. To save on printing costs, students may draw up their own sheets and cut them up.

Demonstrate how to set up for the game. Deal out four cards face down in a row. Add a second card to the card on the far left and the card on the far right. You will now have four piles, one at each end with two cards, and two in the middle with one card each. The two piles on each end will only be used if necessary.

Divide the rest of the deck between the two players, putting the cards in front of each player, face down, in a pile. Let each player pick four cards from the top of his or her pile.

The players then turn over the two cards in the middle and get rid of their piles of cards by placing cards on the two middle piles. The rule for placing a card is that it must come in sequence before or one after the one showing. So, for months of the year, if August is showing in the middle pile, July or September may be put down on top. As cards are being laid down, players take more cards from their private decks, but never have more than four cards in their hands at any time. If neither player has a card to lay down, both can turn one card from each pile at the two ends (those piles with two cards each) so that the game can continue until one player has no more cards in his hand or private pile. If there are no more extra cards in the outside piles, and none of the players has a suitable card to lay down, the player with the fewest cards in his or her private deck wins.

This game will allow players to see words repeatedly and learn how to spell them.

Sequences set up

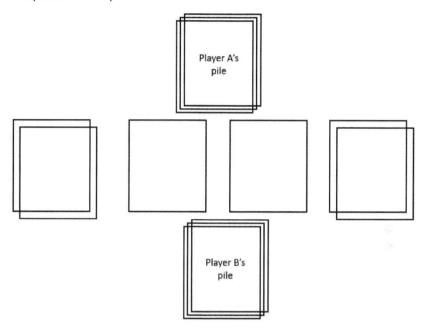

**Language to use with this game**     Use with days of the week, months of the year and numbers that are written out as words so that students see and learn spellings. Use also with any vocabulary words, for spelling, the rule being the sequence of the alphabet. For example, if the word 'unnecessary' is showing face up, then any word starting with a v or a t may be played on it. For the game to work, use no more than 12 different letters in sequence (there will be 4 cards for each), up to 48 different words for higher levels, or 12 words repeated 4 times for beginners. See the examples provided in the appendix: Sequences–Months of the Year.pdf, Sequences–Vocabulary.pdf and Sequences–Vocabulary-Blank.pdf.

**Shopping List Memory Game**

| | |
|---|---|
| Category | Step 2 speaking drill |
| Group size | Divide into small groups of six |
| Level | Beginner to lower intermediate |
| Materials | Optional use of pictures |
| Preparation | None |

**How to play**     Place vocabulary picture cards in a pile. Player 1 takes a card and lays it down, naming the picture or making a sentence about it, as required. Player 2 picks out another card and lays it down next to player 1's picture. Player 2 repeats the required sentence, adding his or her chosen item to the list, and so on, with the list getting longer and longer, for example:

Player 1: 'In my trolley I have got some milk.'
Player 2: 'In my trolley I have got some milk and some chocolate.'
Player 1/3 etc.: 'In my trolley I have got some milk, some chocolate and some oranges.'

If using pictures makes this game too easy, then rely on memory alone.

**Language ideas**                 This game is adaptable to a multitude of language uses, for example:
* There is …/There are … In my wardrobe there are socks, there are shoes, there is a dress, there are shirts, there is a scarf etc.
* Her name is …/His name is …
* She's a …/He's a …
* She likes …/She does not like …
* Playing sports: He plays golf/She plays tennis/He goes horse riding/She windsurfs, etc.

Past tense:
* Yesterday I ate milk, chocolate, pizza, etc.

## Simon Says

| Category | Step 1 listening drill |
|---|---|
| Group size | Any |
| Level | Beginner to intermediate |
| Materials | None |
| Preparation | None |

Simon Says is highly adaptable, can be great fun and is challenging.
     The classic version of Simon Says, for those who do not know the game, is as follows. The teacher starts off as 'Simon' and gives the players instructions they must follow, but only if Simon says so. For example:

- 'Simon says touch your nose.' ['Simon' touches his nose.] All players must touch their nose.
- 'Simon says touch your feet.' ['Simon' touches his feet.] All players must touch their feet.
- 'Touch your head.' ['Simon' touches his head.] However, players must not touch their heads because Simon didn't say so.

In the classic version, any players who touched their head would be out, so as soon as you find that most people are out you restart the game with everyone playing again.

### Grammar version
Players listen to sentences and respond according to the tense. Define which tenses to act on and which to ignore, for example, act on the simple past and the present perfect only. The teacher says: 'I went to the park. Touch your nose.' Students would touch their nose because this sentence is past simple. The teacher says 'I am eating a cake. Touch your leg.' Students don't move since the tense used is neither the simple past nor the present perfect. Use this idea with any grammar. It's a good speaking drill for students too, but put them in small groups and give weaker students an easier grammar point to work on or the game will be too tricky since the student won't be able to think up sentences quickly.

### Fun action version
For players with a good command of the language, and once they have got Simon Says down pat, complicate the game to keep them on their toes. In this version, Simon says two things at once, for example: 'Simon says raise your hand and Simon says touch your leg.' The players must raise their hand and touch their leg. 'Simon says eat ice-cream and touch your nose.' The players must eat ice cream but not touch their nose because Simon did not say so.

### Advanced version
And here is a third, even more complicated version – you may have to rehearse being Simon for this one! When Simon says to do something, the players have to keep doing it until Simon specifically asks them to stop. In the meantime, Simon continues to make other requests. For example:
- Simon says touch your head.
- Simon says touch your shoulder and Simon says stick your tongue out.

- Simon says spin around and shout 'jump'.

At this point the players should be spinning round with one hand on their head and the other on their shoulder, sticking their tongue out, but they should not shout 'jump' as Simon did not say to do so.

Simon then continues with:

- Simon says stop touching your head and rub your stomach instead.

Players must stop touching their heads but should not rub their stomachs, as Simon did not say so.

I'm sure you get the picture. This game can really be a lot of fun and the trick is for you as Simon to keep the pace up and link the commands rapidly so your players' attention is absolutely riveted on listening to your every word!

There is nothing to prevent you playing until you have a winner – the better you get at being Simon, the sooner you will trick everyone into making a mistake and have a victor fairly quickly, and before those who are out have time to get bored. So that it is easy for you to see who is still in the game, have those who are out sit down.

### Simon Says speaking variant

Allow your players to be Simon. Have several Simons at once, as while one Simon is giving a command the other can be thinking of the next one – this ensures the pace is fast and furious, which it needs to be to make this game really fun.

### Solve It

| | |
|---|---|
| Category | Writing and speaking drill |
| Group size | Any |
| Level | Intermediate to advanced |
| Materials | None |
| Preparation | None |

Play in small groups for greater engagement. Two players, who already understand the game, open with one of them making a statement such as 'I'm going away for the weekend and I'm going to take a saucepan with me.' This sentence will be repeated throughout the game so make sure it contains the verb tense you are studying.

The second player continues with: 'I'm going away for the weekend and I'm going to take a saucepan and a notebook with me.'

The next student follows, repeating the sentence so far and adding an item. For the item to be accepted, it must begin with the last letter of the previous item on the list, so here, for example, kettle. However, the other players don't know this link, and have to work out why their answers are being rejected or accepted. Go around the circle with each student attempting to add an item. When you complete the full circle, the first player adds another item, which will provide further clues if no one has guessed the link by this point.

Play usually continues until everyone has caught on to the game, but I'd say stop well before this because it can be humiliating to the one who didn't get it. He or she will feel silly and no doubt hate this activity.

Other than making links via letters, use other criteria to link things together, for example, all items packed must be hard. Therefore the saucepan would be fine, but not a sleeping bag. Other links could be things that are soft, manmade, from nature, alive, smelly, small enough to fit into your pocket, or cold.

**Speed Drill**

| | |
|---|---|
| Category | Step 2 speaking drill |
| Group size | Any |
| Level | Beginner to intermediate |
| Materials | None |
| Preparation | Decide on the sentences you will use for this drill |

Write a sentence using a new grammatical structure that you are teaching and bring two students up to the front to demonstrate. Tell the students to learn the sentence by heart and cover it up or erase it. Give each student a couple of trial runs. Next, on the word 'go', the two students say the sentence out loud, from memory, and try to finish it first with no mistakes. This helps students speak faster as well as drilling grammar. Repeat the demonstration with two different students if you feel it necessary and then let the class divide up into groups of three – two players and one referee. Provide several sentences to work with, each one using the same new grammar, or if you are using this game for revision then use different sentence forms. After each round, the referee becomes a speaker, so students are not always competing against the same person. After five minutes the referee from each group moves to another group, again so that students can vary whom they compete against.

Referees can award two points to the winner and one point to the loser if he or she completes the sentence with no mistakes. This gives a reason for the slower person to finish the sentence too. Students keep a mental note of their points as they circulate around the class. At the end, the two students with the most points can play against each other once for fun in front of the others.

## Spell And Speak

| Category | Spelling |
| --- | --- |
| Group size | Any |
| Level | Beginner to advanced |
| Materials | None |
| Preparation | Decide which words you wish to focus on |

Put players into teams and spell out a word such as 'l-i-g-h-t' or 'b-o-u-g-h-t'. As soon as a student has identified the word, he or she knocks on his or her desk and gives you the answer, gaining points if correct. With more advanced players this is quite a good game to highlight certain words, such as 'bow', which can be pronounced in two different ways, with different meanings, and which can be a noun and a verb.

Also use this game to draw attention to words that have silent letters (as in light and bought) or that sound the same but have different spellings (such as whine and wine, heel and heal, flour and flower whether and weather, or that rhyme but have different spelling patters, such as den and when, graph and staff), or words that are frequently misspelled (recommend, apartment, principle/principal, practice/practise or exercise).

Give a homework assignment where each person prepares a list of three words that he or she thinks are difficult to spell. Divide into teams and play Spell and Speak, each team selecting its own words. Each team member takes a turn at saying a word for the other team to spell. Award a point to the teams for correct spelling. Team members write words on the board simultaneously, which you check as you go along.

With small groups, students can spell words out loud rather than writing them down, which is harder.

Advanced students will get more out of the game if you tell them to prepare a list of words for homework. Give them some examples of good words to use, such as words with silent letters or strange spellings. With business students, include useful and frequently misspelled words such as recommend, necessary, amendment, fulfil, referral and unnecessary.

## Spelling Challenge

| | |
|---|---|
| Category | Spelling |
| Group size | Small groups |
| Leve | Beginner to advanced |
| Materials | Board game included in printable Appendix |
| Preparation | Print one board per group and prepare a list of words |

Use the document Spelling-Challenge.pdf for words of your choice. This is adaptable for any level of spelling difficulty. It may be tailored to business groups using words such as marketable, redundant and commercial, or use it for beginners with basic words.

The teacher calls out a word and players have 30 seconds to write it out. The teacher then writes the word for students to check their spelling. If correct, the player moves forwards by the number of letters in the word.

Spelling Challenge

Spell the word given and move the number of letters forward on the board.

Move back the number of letters if you spell the word wrong!

www.teachingenglishgames.com

If incorrect, the player moves back that number of letters, except if he or she is already at the start.

If necessary, the teacher's role can be given to a student to allow the teacher to be getting on with something else. Another way to free up the teacher is to allow dictionaries, but only for checking purposes once the word has been attempted. Students may also think up words for the other players to spell as the game goes along, and this is a good idea for high-level students who need a challenge.

## Spontaneous Sentence

| Category | Step 5 speaking |
|---|---|
| Level | Upper intermediate to advanced |
| Group size | Any |
| Materials | None |
| Preparation | None |

One student starts a sentence with a word. The next student adds a word and so on until a sentence is constructed. Have one student write the sentence as it is formed on the board for all to see. Specify whether contributions are to be random or to be given in order. This works for small groups only, so for larger classes form teams and have two or three sentences being created simultaneously.

If students need prompting, write parts of speech on the board to help them, for example verb, noun, pronoun, adjective, adverb, conjunctive and preposition.

## Stop

| Category | Step 3 writing drill vocabulary game |
|---|---|
| Group size | Any, played in small groups of four to six |
| Level | Beginner to intermediate |
| Materials | None |
| Preparation | None |

Each player draws a chart with five or six columns, each with a heading, such as numbers, names, countries, animals, clothes, professions, TV shows, food, fruits, things they would like to have, etc. Ensure that students have been introduced to the essential vocabulary for the headings you choose.

One of the players starts the game by calling out the letters of the alphabet. The player next to him or her randomly calls out 'Stop!' The person giving the letters of the alphabet has to stop on the last letter that was spoken, and everyone writes down an item in each category starting with that letter until one player finishes, calls 'Stop!' again and everyone else has to stop writing, whether finished or not.

Give time limits so that the game does not drag on. If no one has said 'Stop!' after two minutes, perhaps because everyone is having difficulty thinking up words beginning with the chosen letter, say stop yourself. Repeat the game with someone else reciting the alphabet and the person next to him or her saying 'Stop.'

Continue for a few rounds and then quickly review the answers, awarding a point for each correct word written. If someone has a word that no one else has, award double points for being original. Have all the players call out their answers so all the students hear the vocabulary repeatedly. Students can tick off their words when they are called out. Let players do their own scoring, although it's not even necessary to ask for scores since this can be humiliating for the weaker students.

Here is an example of a player's chart.

| Animals | Countries or continents | Professions | Colours | Food |
|---|---|---|---|---|
| Panda | Poland | Priest | Purple | Pea |
| Snake | South America | Singer | Scarlet | Sauce |

Adults, teens and children love this game as it is a challenge. Adults may enjoy playing it with niche or general knowledge topics such as car manufacturers and models, fashion labels, shops, cities, plants, composers and musicians, and politicians. If using names, the pronunciation should be English.

**Story Dominoes**

| Category | Step 5 speaking fluency |
|---|---|
| Group size | Small groups of 3 to 6 players per group |
| Level | Lower intermediate to advanced |
| Materials | Dominoes you or the students make (it is easy to do) |
| Preparation | Providing words for the dominoes |

Write a selection of words on small pieces of card to make up a set of dominoes. You need one set per group of students. Choose vocabulary relevant to a theme you are studying or would like to revise.

Here are example domino words for a fantasy story: castle, witch, princess, wand, fairy, prince, magic carpet, dark forest, cave, deep well, monster, lion, queen, king, army, ring, broomstick, mountain, lake, giant, elf, girl, boy, path and gold.

For business students or adults who seem serious, use words such as meeting, executive, sales manager, sales targets, clipboard, overhead projector, PowerPoint presentation, and so on. This way, students will be using vocabulary they feel to be relevant to their needs. With teenagers, a story focused around films, clothing, going on a date or the life of a pop star or actor might appeal. If in doubt, ask your students what they want to make up a story about and let them come up with the core words for the dominoes. Use the same set of dominoes for each group because it will be fun to see how differently the stories turn out.

**How to play**    The group shuffles and deals out the domino word cards. The first player selects a card from his or her pile, places it on the table and makes up the first line of a story using the word on the domino. The next student in the circle adds any one of his or her domino cards and continues the story. Continue until all players have used up their dominoes. The group can then tell their version of the story to another group and vice versa. As a guide, for a group of 6, give out 24 dominoes. Each student will then have four turns. This is long enough, or the task of telling the story to other groups afterwards will be difficult.

**Story Memory Game**

| Category | Step 5 speaking fluency |
|---|---|
| Group size | Groups of six |
| Level | Beginner to intermediate |
| Materials | A story chopped up into sentences |
| Preparation | Choose a story |

Divide students into groups of six. Give each student a line of the story. The first player reads out the first line. The second player must remember it, repeat it, and add his or her line. The third player repeats the first two lines and adds his or her line, and so on. Keep the sentences short so that they are easy to remember and use a tense or grammar point that you would like to reinforce in your current teaching. For beginners, use children's stories, or make up something suitably easy, such as describing their daily routine.

## Storytelling

| Category | Step 5 speaking fluency |
|---|---|
| Group size | Any |
| Level | Beginner to advanced |
| Materials | Several stories |
| Preparation | Find stories in the local library, online, or write them |

As always, explain the purpose of the activity, which is to tell stories for increased fluency. You may also be revising a particular tense, usually the past, but one can tell stories in the future too.

Divide the class into pairs and distribute a selection of stories. Four or so should be sufficient. Use stories from the news, from passages in textbooks, from history books, which are always a great source, or from novels, movies, cartoons, biographies and so on. Alternatively, set homework before completing this task where students each write a story, such as a summary of a favourite novel or film. Correct the stories and use them in class.

Let students work in pairs, telling the story you have given them to each other. At this stage, the students working in pairs have the same story as their partner, as the idea is that they become proficient at telling it. Once you feel that most students are confident in telling their story, you collect them in, mix up the pairs and let students tell their stories to each other. The listener has to give a summary of the story after hearing it, or answer a question about it that the storyteller can ask, so that he or she has a reason to listen to the tale. Swap the students around and repeat. Swap again, and this time allow a time limit of one or two minutes only, so that students have to tell their stories really quickly.

Another idea for storytelling is to have specified storytellers and listeners. Working with a small group of listeners, each storyteller tells only a part of his or her story. The listeners then have a time limit to interview their storytellers to glean as much information about what happens as possible. Then, the listeners get together in groups and try to piece together the whole story, which they then tell to their storyteller, who says whether they are correct or not. This could work well with a multi-level class.

Ideas to help prompt the creation of stories could be movies, your life, your wildest dreams, your work, a picture, an article or newspaper headline, the journey of an object ... who knows how many hands a pen, for example, could pass through! Any small starting point that can trigger your students' imaginations is all it takes. For students who don't seem able or willing to make things up, let them recount a book they read, or a film they saw.

## Subject–Verb–Object

| Category | Step 2 speaking drill |
|---|---|
| Group size | Groups of up to 5 students |
| Level | Beginner to intermediate |
| Materials | Sets of subject–verb–object cards |
| Preparation | None if you use one of the sets provided in the Appendix, or have students make the cards in groups in class |

This is a variant of Find the Pairs memory game.

Print out the set of subject–verb–object cards provided in the Appendix. You will find one set already filled in with vocabulary and another that is blank, ready for filling in by students in class, or by you, using the specific vocabulary you would like used in the game. Use card rather than paper so that it is not see-through when placed face down, otherwise the game is too easy.

One third of the cards have an 's' in the corner and show a noun or pronoun. (If you're using pictures of people, use different sexes of individuals or groups so students can drill he, she and they.) The next third show a verb and have 'v' in the corner; the final third have an 'o' in the corner and show an object. You may use any vocabulary that you are learning or wishing to review for these objects. It is better to use pictures rather than words to review vocabulary, but if you want to work on tenses then using words is fine.

When writing out the verbs use the infinitive so that the students have to think about the correct tense themselves rather than just reading off the card. This also allows you to use the same cards for all tenses. However, for beginners, you might want to make things easier at first and use verb cards with the verbs written out in the tense you are drilling. For example, your verb cards might be make/makes, read/reads, eat/eats and so on. Students will in this case have to match the pronoun 'he' with 'eats' and 'they' with 'eat', which helps them focus on adding the -s/-es for he, she and it. If students make their own cards in class this will help them do better in the game and is a good exercise for beginners.

Each small group of students need a set of 15 cards with 5 subjects, 5 verbs and 5 objects. Shuffle the cards and lay them out, face down. Players take it in turns to turn over three cards, the aim being to reveal a subject, verb and object. When this happens, the student makes up a sentence using the three words, and if correct keeps the three cards. Define in advance whether this sentence should make sense (harder) or not (easier). Continue until no cards are left on the table. The winner or winning team is the one with the most cards at the end.

This game lends itself to any tense and any vocabulary.

## Summaries

| Category | Step 6 creative writing |
|---|---|
| Group size | Any |
| Level | Intermediate to advanced |
| Materials | Texts |
| Preparation | Find texts or have students bring them into class |

In this task, students write a summary of a text. Make this more challenging by saying that no points may be left out, yet the text must be as short as possible. Here is an example.

'It is with great pleasure that I write to you concerning our forthcoming meeting on 15th June. I am thoroughly looking forward to discussing the lesser-spotted miniature penguin with you. I shall be bringing along my collection of over three thousand recordings taken during my honeymoon in Ecuador to identify and classify.'

Students compete to write the most concise version of this without leaving out any key points, such as:

'I am pleased to be meeting you on 15th June to discuss Ecuadorian penguins and classify my recordings.'

Alternatively, have fun reversing the activity and making a short sentence into one that is as long-winded as possible.

'Yesterday it was sunny and I had a lovely walk in the park.'

This might be expanded to:

'Earlier this week, yesterday in fact, given the delightful sunny weather that drew me irresistibly outside, I took the time and the opportunity to stroll about the park enjoying a lovely walk.'

GAMES T

## Talk About It

| | |
|---|---|
| Category | Step 5 speaking fluency |
| Group size | Pairs to 30 students |
| Level | Lower intermediate to advanced |
| Materials | None |
| Preparation | Decide on the topics to discuss |

Set up chairs in rows facing each other, so with ten students you would have five on each side. You sit at the end of the rows as timekeeper. The people on your right are talkers and have to talk about a topic for a minute, without stopping. The people on the left are listeners and do not talk at all except to encourage the talkers and provide a word if they get stuck. Allow any kind of topic, serious or funny. Hand out topics for students to talk about, have all students talking about a different topic, all about the same one, or let students choose their own. If you let students talk about topics of their choice, they may have more to say on them; however, forcing students to talk about a topic you select can stretch their imagination and vocabulary. In general, I would say that it is best to give students a choice of topics at the very least, rather than force someone to talk about goldfish when they know nothing about them other than that they swim and are orange.

All the talkers talk at the same time, so you have to accept a certain amount of noise and you cannot control and correct everything that is said. This is a fluency exercise, so errors are to be expected. When the minute is up, the right row moves one seat down and the last person comes to the front, near you, so all students are now talking to different people. The left side never moves. The people on the right talk on the same topic repeatedly so they have a chance to become more and more fluent at expressing themselves.

When everyone gets back to their original spots, ask the listeners what things they would like to review, what struck them about the topics that was funny or helpful or that they disagreed with, and so on. This gives the listeners a chance to contribute and gives value to their listening activity. Then, or in the next lesson, swap listeners and talkers over.

With advanced students, vary the game by giving a two-minute talking period to allow students to go into their topic in more depth.

## Ten Important Sentences With Watermelon

| | |
|---|---|
| Category | Reading |
| Level | Beginner to intermediate |
| Group size | Any |
| Materials | A written passage chopped into pieces |
| Preparation | Find and chop up a written passage into sentences or partial sentences |

This game helps with summarizing, with scanning for meaning, working under pressure, team building and with vocabulary. It also suits students with a tactile learning style.

Divide the class into small teams of three to four students per team maximum. If you are only teaching a small number of students, put them in pairs. Each team or pair sends a representative up to the board, where you have randomly stuck sentences from a reading passage or story. Each team has its own set of jumbled sentences. For beginners, use a whole sentence per piece of paper; for more advanced levels, chop sentences up too.

Students at the board race to put their text in a coherent order, the catch being that a student may only work on the task while he or she can say 'watermelon' constantly without taking a breath.

When the student runs out of breath, he or she sits down and the next student in the team comes up to continue the work. The winners are those who finish ordering their sentence or passage first.

## Tests And Exams

| | |
|---|---|
| Category | Step 3 writing drill |
| Group size | Any |
| Level | Beginner to advanced |
| Materials | None |
| Preparation | Prepare clear instructions |

Instead of writing your own test or exam each week, have the students write them for each other. The first task is for students to each write five or ten questions based on the previous week's lessons, along with an answer sheet. You collect these and correct any errors. Students rewrite their questions without any errors and bring their tests into the next class. Now, they pair up, and each student does the another one's test. Then they mark each other's work. This process reinforces grammar, which is tested much more efficiently than passively answering set questions, as it requires the students to think for themselves. Students will also enjoy correcting each other; this will boost their confidence as everyone has a chance to be teacher as well as student.

For contingency, if you find that some students do not hand in their work, take some extra copies of one student's test and have that ready with an answer sheet to give to students who come unprepared.

## Things

| Category | Step 6 creative writing with reading |
|---|---|
| Group size | Students are divided into small groups of five to six players |
| Level | Intermediate to advanced |
| Materials | A list of 'things' |
| Preparation | Write the 'things' |

Write a list of provocative 'things', such as things you should not say to your mother, things you should not wear to a wedding, things that go bump in the night, things that can get you arrested, things that you should never put in an oven and so on. These can be listed on paper or printed on card and cut into individual cards.

Each small group of students has the list of 'things' and one student acting as a reader. Starting with the first 'thing you should never do', each student in the group writes down his or her idea of what that thing is, without the others seeing. For example, the 'thing' could be 'things you should never say to your mother'. Students each write a suggestion, such as 'You are looking old.' Students then hand their comment over to the group's reader, who shuffles the ideas and reads out each comment. The other players have to match the comment with the person who wrote it, with only one guess each. If a match is made successfully, the person identified gets a minus point for that round and the person making the correct match gets a point.

Ask the students to come up with a list of 'things' for this game for homework, which they then give to you to allow you to prepare the cards in advance and correct any errors.

### *Variations*

Other ideas for this game include:
- Tell me something about rainy days.
- Tell me something about chocolate.
- Tell me about something furry, etc.
- How do you kill time?

Alternatively, you could ask the students to about a topic of discussion and to tell you about people who drop litter, park on the pavement, work away from home, never marry, are married but don't want children (be careful with topics like this), want a pet dog or cat, don't pay tax, eat horse meat, over-eat, smoke even though they know it might kill them, speed, mug old ladies, think that we should all be equal, are always checking their phones for messages.

*To stop students from feeling concerned about giving away sensitive viewpoints, let everyone hand in their answers on paper. Then the class listens to all the different responses being read out anonymously. It's an interesting way to see how others think without getting personal.*

## Things We Do

| Category | Step 2 speaking drill |
|---|---|
| Level | Beginner to intermediate |
| Group size | Any |
| Materials | None |
| Preparation | None |

This is a verb review game where the teacher gives a category and the students come up with sentences using all the associated verbs they can think of. For example, the teacher says 'housework' and the students make sentences, either in a specific tense, using a specific structure or freely, according to whether you want this to be a grammar drill or a freer speaking activity.

**Time Bomb**

| | |
|---|---|
| Category | Step 2 speaking drill |
| Level | Beginner to intermediate |
| Group size | Divide into small groups |
| Materials | A wind up timer is optional |
| Preparation | Decide on the questions you will ask |

This is a great game to use for any grammar or language structure, from a basic repetitive drill to free questions. You do need a timer of some sort, preferably one that ticks. Wind up the timer and give it to a student. Ask that student a question, the student answers and then passes the timer on. The student holding the timer when it stops loses a life. For beginners, ask the same type of question over and over again, such as: 'Do you like bananas?' 'Do you like eggs?' 'Do you like cooking?' Students reply: 'Yes I do.' 'No I don't.' Drill any grammar in this way. If you have a large class, split it into smaller groups and give each group a timer. Alternatively, if you do not have a timer, let groups pass an object round. When you clap, the people holding the object have to do a forfeit (see Forfeits for ideas) or lose a life.

**Tongue Twisters**

| | |
|---|---|
| Category | Step 5 speaking fluency |
| Group size | Any |
| Level | Beginners to advanced |
| Materials | None |
| Preparation | Bring some tongue twisters |

Classic tongue twisters to have fun with are included below and in a separate word document so that you can edit it as you like and print off what you need.

*Ideas for use*
- Have fun trying to say these quickly to encourage students to speak faster and more fluently.
- Use them as forfeits for other games.
- Try them in Relay Race.
- Give out the tongue twisters as anagrams and let students work out the sentences.

- Dictate the tongue twister in a monotone with no punctuation and let the class work out the punctuation and meaning.

And here are the tongue twisters.

Peter Piper picked a peck of pickled peppers, a peck of pickled peppers Peter Piper picked.

She sells seashells on the seashore. The shells she sells are seashells.

I wish to wish the wish you wish to wish, but if you wish the wish the witch wishes, I won't wish the wish you wish to wish.

Betty bought butter, but the butter was bitter, so Betty bought better butter to make the bitter butter better.

Fuzzy Wuzzy was a bear, Fuzzy Wuzzy had no hair, Fuzzy Wuzzy wasn't very fuzzy, was he?

If a black bug bleeds black blood, what colour blood does a blue bug bleed?

It's not the cough that carries you off, it's the coffin they carry you off in!

I saw a saw that could out saw any saw I ever saw before.

Any noise annoys an oyster but a noisy noise annoys an oyster more.

More advanced tongue twisters:

**Mr See and Mr Saw**
Mr See owned a saw. And Mr Soar owned a seesaw. Now See's saw sawed Soar's seesaw before Soar saw See, which made Soar sore. Had Soar seen See's saw before See sawed Soar's seesaw; See's saw would not have sawed Soar's seesaw.

### The bear and the hare

I cannot bear to see a bear bear down upon a hare. When bare of hair he strips the hare, right there I cry, 'Forbear!'

### Theofilis Thistle (this is good for French speakers who have trouble with 'th')

Theofilis Thistle, the successful thistle sifter, one day while sifting a sieve full of unsifted thistles, thrust three thousand thistles through the thick of his thumb. Now if Theofilis Thistle, the successful thistle sifter, one day while sifting a sieve full of unsifted thistles, thrust three thousand thistles through the thick of his thumb, see that you while sifting a sieve full of unsifted thistles, thrust not three thousand thistles through the thick of your thumb.

### The tree toad

A tree toad loved a she-toad who lived up in a tree. He was a two-toed tree toad but a three-toed toad was she. The two-toed tree toad tried to win the three-toed she-toad's heart, for the two-toed tree toad loved the ground that the three-toed tree toad trod. But the two-toed tree toad tried in vain. He couldn't please her whim. From her tree toad bower with her three-toed power the she-toad vetoed him.

### Treasure Hunt

| | |
|---|---|
| Category | Step 1 listening and writing |
| Group size | Any |
| Level | Adaptable to any level |
| Materials | Any small objects |
| Preparation | Students hide objects |

This is a listening activity, ideal for learning prepositions and classroom objects and furniture, where the teacher describes the whereabouts of a hidden object. Students listen and try to be the first to find the object.

### *Variation*

Extend the activity to a writing task where students write out directions to find an object in class.

Students place their instructions all around the room, on the walls, the desks and the floor. Only one of the instructions leads to the hidden object.

The object does not even need to be hidden – it could be in plain sight, but nobody knows what it is. Bear in mind that objects cannot be hidden in people's bags or amongst personal possessions.

**Triangles Talking Point**

| Category | Step 5 speaking fluency |
|---|---|
| Group size | Divide into small groups |
| Level | Intermediate to advanced |
| Materials | None |
| Preparation | Decide on the three points of each triangle |

Draw a triangle on the board and write one objects in each corner, for example, lorry, bus and car, or something related to the subject you are studying. Then ask students which is the best, and why? You'll get some very interesting answers.

**True Or False**

| Category | Step 1 listening vocabulary for beginners |
|---|---|
| Group size | All sizes |
| Level | Beginner |
| Materials | Pictures or objects |
| Preparation | Prepare the statements you will make if you cannot think of things off the cuff |

For basic vocabulary work, name an item or make a statement, and the class says whether it is true or false. For example, point to a picture of an apple and say 'This is a pear.' The class must say 'False.' Hold a pen under a chair and say 'The pen is under the chair.' The class must say 'True,' and so on.

**True Or False Questions**

| Category | Step 2 speaking drill |
|---|---|
| Group size | Any |
| Level | Beginner to lower intermediate |
| Materials | None |
| Preparation | Think about the questions you will use for the drill |

This game is a question drill game suitable for beginners to lower intermediate. It is excellent for drilling any type of question form and tense.

You need to imagine something for the students to guess what it is through asking questions. For example, to work on present continuous, you imagine an outfit you are wearing. Use picture cards of clothes to help students think of clothing items if necessary. The students ask in unison, 'What are you wearing?' You reply, for example, 'I'm wearing a red hat.' Each class member decides whether he or she thinks this is true or false. Everyone stands, and whoever thinks it is true puts a hand up. Whoever thinks it is false keeps both hands down. Those who get it wrong are out and have to sit down. Continue until the class has discovered the full outfit and see which students are still in the game. Those who are out still ask the questions in unison with the class, but they cannot play.

Play with any language or as above, but change the vocabulary or language to suit your needs.

Here is a past tense example: 'What did you eat last night?' 'I ate spaghetti.'

Here is a future (using present continuous) example: 'Where are you going for your holiday?' 'I'm going to Spain.'

To personalize this activity, have students prepare a scenario for homework and then in the next lesson play again. Students come up to the front in turn and you play the games as described above, using their scenarios.

## Typhoon

| | |
|---|---|
| Category | Step 2 speaking drill |
| Group size | 3 to 18 players, up to 30 players at a stretch |
| Level | Beginner to intermediate |
| Materials | None |
| Preparation | Think about the questions you will use for the drill |

Divide your class into three or more teams and draw a grid on the board and an identical grid on a piece of paper. Label the top row and left-hand column with numbers and letters, or with vocabulary, as below. Numbers and letters are good for beginners learning the alphabet. On the paper version, in a few of the grids write a T, and then fill in a random score in each remaining empty grid square. The scores can vary from zero to several million. Stick to simple numbers for beginners and use more variety with the intermediate students.

BOARD VERSION

|  | Chicken | Sheep | Goat | Donkey |
|---|---|---|---|---|
| Horse |  |  |  |  |
| Cow |  |  |  |  |
| Pig |  |  |  |  |

PAPER VERSION

|  | Chicken | Sheep | Goat | Donkey |
|---|---|---|---|---|
| Horse | 10 | T | 300 | 5 |
| Cow | 100 | 500 | T | 400 |
| Pig | T | 200 | 50 | 300 |

Students must answer a question for their team and if correct they choose a square on the grid, such as 'chicken horse' if you are using vocabulary words. You then read out the score for that grid, which in this case is 10 points, and that team wins 10 points for having answered the question correctly. You or a student can be up at the board writing up the team scores. If a student picks a square on the grid that is labelled 'T', the team has the right to wipe out another team's score. This game is more interesting with more than two teams or players.

To finish the game, players can stop once they reach a certain score. For example, if players reach a score of 1,000, they have won.

Once you have played a couple of times and students have the hang of this game, then add variety by increasing the number of squares in the grid and add for example 'S' to steal another team's score and 'D' to double your own score in some of squares.

GAMES U–Z

## Vocabulary Baseball

| | |
|---|---|
| Category | Speaking fluency |
| Group Size | Smaller groups |
| Level | Lower intermediate and upwards |
| Materials | Vocabulary lists, taught in advance; prizes (optional!) |
| Preparation | Pre-teach words and prepare vocabulary lists |

This game takes minimal preparation time, but the vocabulary must have been taught in previous lessons. Compile a vocabulary list, or cards, for the 'pitcher'. Easy words are marked 'single', difficult words are 'double' and harder words are 'triple'. If you have bonus challenge words, they can be 'home runs'.

**How to play**     This game can be played as a drill or for fluency. If playing as a drill, use the same structure over and over; if playing for fluency, allow any kinds of sentences.

Divide the class into two teams. Push desks to the sides. Tell students where the first, second, third and home plates are. The students take turns 'batting' and the other team takes turns 'pitching' or reading the words.

The batter requests a single, double or triple (or home run if you have decided to allow them). The pitcher, with the help of the team if you like, picks a word and calls it out to the batter. The batter gives a definition and uses the word in a sentence.

If the umpire (usually the teacher) decides that the batter is correct, he or she advances a base. Any other players on base also advance. When a batter reaches 'home base', the team gets a point. If the definition or usage in the sentence is incorrect, then the batter is out. Three outs mean the teams change places.

You may choose how many innings to play. Three innings is a good number, but it will depend on how large your teams are. The team with the most points wins a pre-determined prize.

**Vocabulary Picture Hunt**

| Category | Spelling |
|---|---|
| Level | Beginner to lower intermediate |
| Group size | Any |
| Materials | Pictures from magazines |
| Preparation | None once you have found the pictures |

Find pictures containing vocabulary you want to teach or revise. These are not picture flashcards, but pictures of scenes that contain your vocabulary. For example, one of your words might be coffee machine, and this could be found in a picture of an office interior. Write these vocabulary words on the board while students copy them down. Number your pictures and spread them about the room. Give a couple of minutes for students to look for the objects on the board and find them in the pictures. When a student has found an object in a picture, he or she can write the picture number next to the word on his or her paper. The first five students to finish are the winners.

Think of magazines such as home decor magazines for household objects or furniture, fashion magazines for clothing and accessories, *Hello* magazine or equivalent for scenes of people's houses, sporting publications for various sports, business magazines for technical vocabulary on computing and telecommunications, or specialist subject magazines, such as health or engineering, relevant to your group. Free catalogues from large chain stores are filled with a wealth of pictures, as are free brochures and leaflets.

**Vocabulary Scavenger Hunt Listening**

| Category | Listening |
|---|---|
| Level | Beginner to intermediate |
| Group size | Any |
| Materials | Passages of text either pre-recorded or to be read out |
| Preparation | Choose a selection of listening passages with related questions or gap-fills |

Use this game as a general listening comprehension or for specific grammar as a listening gap-fill exercise.

Place several listening devices such as portable CD players with speakers at different places in the room. If you do not have any equipment and students do not want to use their own, then have a student at each 'listening post' read out the passages instead. The advantage of using native speakers' recorded versions is that students get used to hearing English from around the world spoken with varied pronunciation.

Students have a time limit to go around all the listening stations and find the answers to their questions, or fill in the missing words in their gap fills. The different passages may be parts of a story that are broken up into sections that students must piece it together again. The listening passage should be played or read from start to finish, then rewound and played again as needed. Students cannot stop the passage halfway through if they show up in the middle of it. It's all part of the game.

## Vocabulary Scavenger Hunt Reading

| | |
|---|---|
| Category | Skimming/reading passages for vocabulary and/or grammar |
| Level | Beginner to intermediate |
| Group size | Any |
| Materials | Reading passages and a list of words to find |
| Preparation | Choosing a reading passage and listing words to find |

The purpose of this activity is to scan passages for words and for vocabulary review. Find a reading passage that suits the level of your students and select a number of terms from the passage. If you are using a textbook, look no further, and use this activity with reading passages. Each student needs a copy of the reading passage and the list of words to find, which can be on the board. Set a time limit and let students race to find all the words in the passage, circling or highlighting them as they skim through. With higher-level students, ask them to state the function of the word in the context of the passage, i.e. is it being used as a noun, a verb or an adverb? and so on. Students can be given the infinitive of verbs and told to find all occurrences of that verb in the text, regardless of tense. (This can be useful for highlighting irregular past tenses.)

## Vocabulary Repetition

| | |
|---|---|
| Category | Step 2 speaking drill |
| Level | Beginner |
| Group size | Groups of up to eight students |
| Materials | None |

| Preparation | None |
| --- | --- |

This is an excellent game for learning new vocabulary. It's very easy, non-threatening and provides students the opportunity to get their chops around new terms. Seat adults in a circle if possible, in groups of up to eight. Start the game by saying, for example, 'one hat'. Each student repeats these words until they go full circle around the group. Now add a new vocabulary item – 'one hat, two gloves' – and again repeat this full circle round the group. Add a third item and so on. Use with any vocabulary or to drill short sentences using specific grammar.

With larger groups, pass round more words at a time so students are fully occupied listening to the next word or sentence coming to them. As a variant, use vocabulary flashcards as prompts, which are passed around the circle.

## What Or Who Am I?

| Category | Step 5 speaking fluency |
| --- | --- |
| Group size | Any |
| Level | Intermediate to advanced |
| Materials | None |
| Preparation | Find product advertisements or think of people who can be mystery characters the others must guess |

Let your students think of a product that they have seen advertised recently. Give them English magazines to flip through briefly, if necessary. With students in pairs, give a minute's time limit for one student in each pair to figure out the other student's product by asking questions. Students can ask anything about the product, but not what it is! Before you start, brainstorm for suitable questions. When the minute is up, blow a whistle, and students must swap roles. After that minute is up, blow the whistle again, and students swap pairs. Be on hand to help students form questions and listen for common errors to correct at the end.

A variation on how to play is to allow five students to think up a mystery character. The other students divide into groups and have two minutes to interview the mystery character to find out who he or she is. When the two minutes are up, give a signal; then the groups move on until they have been round all the mystery people. At the end, see which group has guessed the most characters correctly. The larger your class, the more mystery characters you would have. You ideally want a ratio of one mystery person to three to five students asking questions.

### *Variation*

A variant of this game, from Robert Goulston, focuses on four question types:
1. Yes/No
Example: 'Are you going to London today?'
2. Open
Example: 'What do you think of the president?'
3. Tags
Example: 'It's raining isn't it?'
4. Indirect
Example: 'Could you tell me where the station is, please?'

In small teams, students think of a famous personality, dead or alive, and come up with four questions, one of each type. Teams swap questions. Each team asks the questions and tries to guess the other team's personality. Do this in small groups to increase student participation and talking time.

## Which One Has Gone?

| | |
|---|---|
| Category | Step 2 speaking drill |
| Group size | All class sizes but best in small groups |
| Level | Beginner |
| Materials | Picture flashcards or words |
| Preparation | None |

Put up a set of picture cards on the board and ask the students to close their eyes. Take away one of the cards on the board and ask 'Which one has gone?' Students now open their eyes and identify the missing picture as quickly as possible.

Take away more than one picture at a time if you wish. To make this game more challenging, move the pictures around in between goes (as long as you keep up the pace so as not to waste time!). Let the winner of each round ask the question and take the picture(s) away to give the others a chance to answer.

With a large class, divide it into groups; give each group a set of pictures, which students lay on their tables. You will then need a caller for each group. Everyone can have a turn at this.

## Why?

| | |
|---|---|
| Category | Speaking |
| Level | Intermediate and up |
| Group size | Any – divide into small groups with a big class |
| Materials | None |
| Preparation | None |

This game is played with or without pictures and encourages creative thinking and general language. The teacher, or a student, makes a statement such as 'He is hot. Why?' Students invent a plausible answer such as 'He is hot because the sun is shining.'

Pictures are fun way in which to spark the imagination and any magazine can be used. For example, using a picture of a man, ask 'Why is he wearing this shirt in particular?' Students use their imagination to come up with something like it was the only clean one he had left!

Thanks to Olga Benedik in the Ukraine for sending me this idea.

## Word Association

| | |
|---|---|
| Category | Speaking for vocabulary revision |
| Level | All intermediate levels |
| Group size | Divide students into pairs or groups of three or four |
| Materials | None |
| Preparation | None |

One student says a word, such as 'elephant', and the next student offers a related word, such as grey, leg or big. Play this in pairs, in small groups, or by dividing the class into teams.

## Word Chains

| | |
|---|---|
| Category | Spelling and vocabulary review |
| Level | Intermediate and up |
| Group size | Any |
| Materials | None |

| Preparation | None |
|---|---|

Divide students in teams with one team member from each team at the board. The team members at the board each write a word. The other team members now make a word chain by finding either a word that rhymes with the word on the board, or a word that starts with the same sound. Teams race to make the longest chain in a given timeframe.

Here is an example: trick. The word try starts with the same tr sound, or prick rhymes with trick. So a chain might look like this: trick, thick, thank, thin, pin, pick, sick, sit, fit, pit, pink, think.

### *Variation*

You can also play be changing one letter in a word. Divide the class into teams. One member from each team writes a word on the board. (Have all teams working simultaneously, not one after another.) Someone else from each team then changes one letter of the word to make a different word. Allow a fixed time limit for this and see which team has the longest chain of words at the end.

Here is an example: coat, coal, foal, foil, toil, soil, sail, nail, bail, ball, fall, call, tall, tale, male, pale, sale.

To make this game easier for lower intermediates, allow two letters to be changed; the order of the letters can be changed as well. Equally, you could allow for a letter to be added or taken away to give more possibilities for finding words.

### Word Chain – Round The Alphabet

| Category | Speaking for vocabulary review |
|---|---|
| Level | Beginner to intermediate |
| Group size | Any |
| Materials | None |
| Preparation | None |

Taking a theme such as countries, students use the letters of the alphabet in order: Afghanistan, Belgium, Congo, Denmark, Ethiopia, etc. Divide a big class into two or more groups so students do not wait forever between turns.

Another method is to play with one big group, but with students in threes, and any one of the three can give an answer when it's their turn. This also helps avoid delays when someone is stuck. If a person takes longer than ten seconds to find an answer, he or she skips a turn and the word moves on to the next person. Subject areas include:

- countries/independent states
- cities
- nouns
- verbs
- adjectives
- adverbs
- food items
- items you can buy
- movies
- names
- famous people
- space
- sports
- jobs

The game will move faster if you ask students to prepare for it for homework. Demonstrate how the game works, and then give students the theme or themes that you will use in the next lesson. General trivia categories usually go down well, as students feel they are learning on two levels: as well as practising their English, they are improving their general knowledge.

This game can be played as a competition – players are 'out' if they cannot think of a word – or as a collaborative game wherein the goal is for each team to make it round the alphabet. Have two teams racing to be the first to complete the task, which is then performed in front of the other team. Using the collaborative method also means more repetition as the team tries to make it from a to z.

**Word Order**

| Category | Step 1 listening drill |
|---|---|
| Group size | 4–30 players divided into small groups |
| Level | Beginner to Intermediate |
| Materials | None |
| Preparation | Prepare sentences that you will jumble |

Read out a short sentence with the word order jumbled up. Students listen and call out the correct order. If students cannot do this quickly, then the sentences are too hard or too varied.

To use this exercise for drilling, stick to sentences with identical structure or grammar such as:

- I gave you a rose.
- He gave me a rose.
- She gave him a rose.
- They gave her a rose.

… and so on. A simpler example is:

- I like biscuits.
- She likes coffee.
- They like jam.

… and so on.

With students in teams, let each team have a few seconds to reply before opening the floor to all teams. A team member can only answer out loud once and then must whisper the answer to another team member instead. This keeps all players involved and prevents one person from giving all the answers.

**Write It Up**

| | |
|---|---|
| Category | Writing drill |
| Group size | Any |
| Level | Beginner to lower intermediate |
| Materials | None |
| Preparation | None |

Divide the class into teams and number the players in each team. Give an example of a sentence that uses the grammar you want to work with, for example, the past simple tense: Yesterday I walked the dog.

Now allow students 15 seconds to think up their own sentence in the simple past. Call out one of the team numbers, say number 3. All the number 3s come quickly to the board and write the sentence they have thought of, such as 'Yesterday I cleaned my teeth.' If the less-able students want to copy from a more advanced classmate, OK – this is not cheating, but a learning experience. Have students make sure the sentences written are correct.

While this has been going on, all class members should be thinking of a new sentence using the same grammar. Call out another team number, say 1; the 1s come up and write their version of the sentence, and so on. Have a rule where no sentence may be repeated on the board.

Use short, simple sentences with beginners. You may also use this game for single words to study vocabulary and spelling.

## Writing Relay

| Category | Step 6 writing drill |
| --- | --- |
| Group size | All sizes divided into teams |
| Level | Beginner to lower intermediate |
| Materials | Class board and several chalks or board pens |
| Preparation | None |

Divide the class into logical teams, according to existing seating. Draw one column per team on the board. Write different letters in each column. One student from each team comes up to the board and writes a word starting with the first letter in the column for his or her team. The second student in the team then comes to the board and adds a second word. The game, or one round of the game, is complete when one team finishes. Students may use dictionaries at their desks, but not at the board.

Here is an example for two teams finding adverbs.

| Team 1 | Team 2 |
| --- | --- |
| a *adoringly* | a *angrily* |
| b *beautifully* | b *bluntly* |
| c *cleverly* | c *cunningly* |
| d *dutifully* | d *dully* |
| ... | ... |

Variations include specifying that the words must be nouns, adverbs, verbs or adjectives. To make this easier for beginners, don't specify letters. However, you probably do want to include a rule that no word can be repeated anywhere on the board.

At the end, award points for the number of words spelled correctly. It is a good idea to let the teams have a chance to correct spelling mistakes they notice before counting up the points. Let students work out what the points are for each team.

## Zip Zap Vocabulary Revision

| | |
|---|---|
| Category | Step 2 speaking drill for vocabulary review |
| Group size | Small group |
| Level | Beginner to lower intermediate |
| Materials | Picture flashcards |
| Preparation | None |

This is a fun vocabulary revision game to play for five minutes. It gives students a chance to stand up and move from their desks, makes the mind alert and gives everyone a chance to say a few words and revise vocabulary. (It is too easy for advanced players, though.)

Players form a circle, each one holding a picture card. In turn, each player stands in the middle of the circle and names the object on his or her card. Each person needs to remember the cards on his or her left and right. Once you have gone round the circle, the first student comes to the middle in turn again, but this time the player in the middle points a finger at one of the players in the circle and says, for example, ZIP–1,2,3,4,5. The student being pointed at must then name the card on his or her left. If the player in the middle says ZAP–1,2,3,4,5, then the student being pointed at must name the picture card on his or her right (all without looking, of course!). If successful, the person in the middle repeats the exercise with another student. If unsuccessful, the student being asked swaps places with the person in the middle.

# PART 3

## JOKES, METAPHORS, RIDDLES, PROVERBS

These jokes came from emails and the Internet – I don't know who the authors are and I don't claim to have made them up myself! I have deliberately stuck to innocent jokes that avoid sensitive issues.

\* \* \*

One day a man was walking in the park and he found a penguin. He was shocked and he didn't know what to do. Finally, he decided to take the penguin to the police station, and told the police officer what had happened.

The police officer said, 'You must take this penguin to the zoo.'

The man said, 'That's a good idea! I will take the penguin to the zoo now.' So he took the penguin to the zoo.

The next day, the police officer was walking in the street and he saw the man with the penguin.

The police officer said, 'Why didn't you take the penguin to the zoo?'

The man said, 'I did. We went to the zoo yesterday, and today we are going to the cinema.'

\* \* \*

There was a man walking in the desert. He didn't have any water to drink and he was really thirsty. Suddenly, he saw a man riding a donkey. He ran to the man and said, 'Water, water! I need water!'

But the man on the donkey said, 'I'm sorry, I haven't got any water. But I have got a lot of ties: blue ties, yellow ties, green ties, every colour. They are very cheap! Would you like to buy one?'

The man said, 'No, I don't want a tie – I need water.' And he continued walking.

A short time later, he saw another man riding a camel. He ran to the man and he said, 'Water, water! I need water!'

But the man on the camel said, 'I'm sorry, I haven't got any water. But I have got a lot of shirts: blue shirts, yellow shirts, green shirts, every colour. They are very cheap! Would you like to buy one?'

The man didn't buy a shirt. He continued walking.

Finally, the man saw a restaurant in the middle of the desert. He ran to the restaurant and said, 'Water, water! I need water!'

But the man at the door said, 'I'm sorry – you can't come in without a shirt and tie.'

\* \* \*

There was a little dog and it was very happy because it was going to go to school for the first time. The little dog's mother kissed the little dog and said, 'Have a good day at school and come straight home afterwards.' Then the little dog went to school.

In the evening, the little dog came home from school. The little dog's mother asked the little dog, 'What did you learn at school today?'

The little dog said, 'We studied foreign languages today.'

His mother was surprised, 'Which foreign language did you study?'

And the little dog said, 'Meow.'

\* \* \*

One Monday morning John was lying in bed. His mother came into the bedroom and said, 'Wake up John! It's time to go to school.'

But John said, 'I don't want to go to school.'

Five minutes later his mother said, 'Wake up John! I've made your breakfast; you must eat it before you go to school.'

But John said, 'I don't want to go to school.'

Five minutes later his mother said, 'Wake up John! If you don't wake up now, you'll be late for school.'

But John said, 'I don't want to go to school.'

His mother said, 'But you have to go to school.'

John said, 'Why do I have to go to school?'

His mother said, 'Because you are a teacher.'

\* \* \*

There was a man who had an accident and hurt his hands, so he had to go to hospital.

The doctor put some bandages on his hands and told him to come back one week later.

When the man came back to the hospital one week later, the doctor took off the bandages. The man asked the doctor, 'Can I play the piano now?'

The doctor said, 'Of course you can play the piano.'

The man said, 'That's unbelievable! I couldn't play the piano before the accident.'

* * *

One day, a man found an old lamp. When he started cleaning it, a genie came out of it.

The genie said, 'I am the genie of the lamp. You have got three wishes. What would you like?'

The man thought about this for a few seconds and then he said, 'Can I have a bottle of whisky?'

Suddenly, there was a loud noise and a big flash, and the man was holding a bottle of whisky.

He opened the bottle and he started drinking the whisky. But after drinking a lot of whisky the bottle was still full. The genie said, 'This is a never-ending bottle of whisky. Drink as much as you want and the bottle will always be full.'

Then the genie said, 'You have got two more wishes. What would you like?'

And the man said, 'Can I have two more bottles of whisky?'

* * *

Tom had been looking for a job for a long time. He finally found one at the zoo. But on his first day his new boss came to him and said: 'We have got a big problem and we need your help! Our gorilla died at the weekend and we need a new gorilla but we haven't got enough money at the moment. You will have to put on this gorilla costume and sit in the gorilla cage. Everyone will think that you are the gorilla.'

Tom wasn't too happy about this, but he needed the job, so he did what his boss wanted.

After a few weeks, Tom began to enjoy being the gorilla. He ran around his cage and he jumped and danced for all the people. In a short time he became the most popular animal in the zoo.

One day he was swinging very high in his cage and suddenly he flew off his branch and fell into the lion's cage. Of course, Tom was afraid, and he began to shout 'Help me! Help me!'

The lion ran, jumped on Tom, and said: 'Shut up, or everyone will lose their jobs!'

* * *

Dave, Kevin and Sharon were driving along the road one day when a policeman stopped Dave's car.

The policeman said, 'I have been waiting here all day and you are the first person I saw wearing a seat belt. I'm going to give you $500 as a reward.'

Dave was very happy and he said, 'Great! Now I can get a driving licence with this money.'

Sharon said, 'And we can buy more alcohol.'

Kevin said, 'Shut up. We mustn't drink in a stolen car.'

\* \* \*

A ship sank and three sailors were stranded on a small island for 20 years. One day, when they were walking on the beach, they found an old lamp. When they cleaned it, a genie came out.

The genie said to them, 'I will do whatever you want. You can have one wish each.'

The first man said, 'I want to go home and see my beautiful wife again.'

The genie clapped his hands and the man disappeared.

The second man said, 'I want to go home and see my beautiful wife again!'

The genie clapped his hands and the man disappeared.

The genie turned to the third man and said, 'What do you want?'

And the third man said, 'Can I have my two friends back?'

\* \* \*

One day, a man came to the hospital with two burnt ears.

The doctor was very surprised to see this and he asked the man what had happened.

The man said, 'I was ironing my clothes when the telephone rang. I thought it the telephone was the iron so I picked it up and I burned my ear.'

'How did you burn the other ear?' the doctor asked.

The man said, 'They called me back.'

\* \* \*

Teacher: Sarah, why are you doing your maths multiplication on the floor?
Sarah: You told me to do it without using tables.

\* \* \*

Teacher: Glenn, how do you spell 'crocodile'?
Glenn: K–r–o–k–o–d–i–a–l.'

Teacher: No, that's wrong.
Glenn: Maybe it is wrong, but you asked me how I spell it.

\* \* \*

Teacher: Donald, what is the chemical formula for water?
Donald: H–I–J–K–L–M–N–O.
Teacher: What are you talking about?
Donald: Yesterday you said it was H to O.

\* \* \*

Teacher: Sam, why do you always get so dirty?
Sam: Well, I'm a lot closer to the ground than you are.

\* \* \*

Teacher: Millie, give me a sentence starting with 'I'.
Millie: I is the …
Teacher: No, Millie … always say, 'I am.'
MILLIE: All right … I am the ninth letter of the alphabet.

\* \* \*

Teacher: Now, Simon, tell me frankly, do you say prayers before eating?
Simon: No, Sir, I don't have to – my mum is a good cook.

\* \* \*

Teacher: Clyde, your composition on 'My Dog' is exactly the same as your brother's. Did you copy his?
Clyde: No, Sir. It's the same dog.

\* \* \*

Teacher: Harold, what do you call a person who keeps on talking when people are no longer interested?
Harold: A teacher

\* \* \*

A factory in Louisiana was recruiting. Dan applied for an engineering position.

Pete applied for the same job. Both applicants had the same qualifications, so they were asked to take a test by the manager.

Upon completion of the test, both men only missed one of the questions. The manager went to Dan and said: 'Thank you for your interest, but we've decided to give the Pete the job.'

Dan asked: 'And why are you giving him the job? We both got nine questions correct. This being Louisiana, and me being a Southern boy, I should get the job.'

The manager said: 'We have made our decision not on the correct answers, but rather on the one question that you both missed.'

Dan then asked: 'And just how would one incorrect answer be better than the other?'

The manager replied: 'Dan, it's like this. On question four, Pete put down "I don't know." You put down "Neither do I."'

\* \* \*

Here's a silly quiz to do in pairs, to find out whether you learn from your mistakes. It's from an email that was being sent around. Give student A the questions and correct answers. Student A asks the first question, and student B answers as he or she sees fit. Student A reads the correct answer and the diagnosis. Student A then continues to question 2.

Q1. How do you put a giraffe into a refrigerator?
Correct answer: Open the refrigerator, put in the giraffe and close the door.
Diagnosis: This question tests whether you tend to do simple things in an overly complicated way.

Q2. How do you put an elephant into a refrigerator?
Incorrect answer: Open the refrigerator, put in the elephant, and close the refrigerator.
Correct answer: Open the refrigerator, take out the giraffe, put in the elephant and close the door.
Diagnosis: This tests your ability to think through the repercussions of your previous actions.

Q3. The Lion King is hosting an animal conference. All the animals attend except one. Which animal does not attend?
Correct answer: The elephant, since it is still in the refrigerator.
Diagnosis: This tests your memory.

OK, even if you did not answer the first three questions correctly, you still have one more chance to show your true abilities.

Q4. There is a river you must cross but it is inhabited by crocodiles. How do you manage it?
Correct answer: You swim across. All the crocodiles are attending the animal conference.
Diagnosis: This tests whether you learn quickly from your mistakes.

According to Anderson Consulting Worldwide, around 90 per cent of the professionals they tested got all questions wrong. But many pre-schoolers got several correct answers.

Anderson Consulting says this conclusively disproves the theory that most professionals have the brains of a four-year-old.

**Metaphors**

Here is a collection of metaphors to use with Call My Bluff Definitions or Pairs. If playing Pairs, use the metaphor and correct definition only. If playing Call My Bluff, the first definition is true while the second and third are false. I really had fun making these up, so your students might enjoy this activity too.

Airhead
- Someone who is disorganized or a bit stupid
- A head with a huge amount of hair
- A capsule that prevents air coming out of a bicycle tyre

Beacon
- Someone who inspires through example
- A ditch
- A species of hunting dog

Black and white
- Things are clear
- A type of chocolate bar
- Fair-skinned people in dark suits

Blanket of snow
- A layer of snow on the ground
- A white blanket
- A blanket with pictures of snow on it

194

Bowels of the building
- In the cellars or lower parts of a building
- In the toilets
- The plumbing system of a building

Cold feet
- When you feel scared to do something
- When you have poor circulation
- When you do something without a warm up

Cold turkey
- When a drug addict has withdrawal symptoms
- The favourite Christmas dish in Britain
- When you feel too scared to do something

Couch potato
- A slob who spends all day watching TV
- A dish made of layers of cheese and potato
- A potato with a long flat shape

Dim view
- When you do not agree with or approve of something
- When your eyesight is suffering
- When you cannot see for lack of sufficient light

Good taste
- When someone likes your style or belongings, they say you have this
- When food is good it has good taste
- When your mother makes your favourite dish

Light conversation
- A chat about fun or trivial things
- A conversation about lighting
- A short conversation or dialogue

Old flame
- An ex-girl or boyfriend

- A fire that has nearly gone out
- The name given to the flame lit at the Olympics

Road hog
- An aggressive drive who takes over the road
- A hog that has been run over
- A type of pig that uses roads to migrate

Room to grow
- Space to allow for inner or physical growth
- A heated room for rapid plant growth
- A room where you meditate and read books on personal development

Rug rat
- A child
- A rat with a lot of fur
- A pet rat

Shades of grey
- When things are not clear
- Sunglasses with grey lenses
- Art work that is mostly made up of grey, black and white

Shady character
- Someone of dubious morals
- A character who makes sun shades
- A person who prefers the shade to the sun

To bite your lip
- To try hard not to say something
- When you need stitches in your lip
- When you are deep in thought and squeeze your lip between your teeth

To come to the point
- To finally say what you mean
- To reach the edge of a cliff where land meets sea
- To decide not to do something after all

To go smoothly
- When things are going well
- When you drive on a road that has no bumps
- The smooth feel of your hair after you have brushed it

To hit a brick wall
- To come up against an insurmountable obstacle
- To replace missing bricks in a brick wall
- To disagree with someone

To spit it out
- To say something
- To find an idea immoral or disgusting
- To spit over a great distance

Warm reception
- When someone is welcoming
- A party given in a warm room
- A wedding reception with a lot of guests

Weighty subject
- An important matter
- A heavy person
- A weighty person wishing to embark on a diet

You could use this same idea with similes.

As cold as ice
- When someone is not welcoming
- When you have a cold
- When your body drops to sub-zero temperatures

Another activity that involves your students and encourages creativity is to ask them to make up their own metaphors or similes and discuss them with other students.

# Riddles

I received these amusing riddles via an email that was being forwarded around the Internet. Use them with the game Match Up. Use crossword puzzles for more cryptic clues and definitions.

Boss
Someone who is early when you are late and late when you are early.

Compromise
The art of dividing a cake in such a way that everybody believes he or she got the biggest piece.

Conference
The confusion of one man multiplied by the number present.

Conference room
A place where everybody talks, nobody listens and everybody disagrees later on.

Criminal
A guy no different from the rest ... except that he got caught.

Dictionary
A place where success comes before work.

Divorce
Future tense of marriage.

Father
A banker provided by nature.

Lecture
An art of transferring information from the notes of the lecturer to the notes of the students without passing through the minds of either.

Life insurance
A contract that keeps you poor all your life so that you can die rich.

## Marriage
An agreement in which a man loses his bachelor degree and a woman gains her masters.

## Nurse
A person who wakes you up to give you sleeping pills.

## School
A place where papa pays and son plays.

## Tears
The hydraulic force by which masculine willpower is defeated by feminine water power.

* * *

1. What do you call a deer with no eyes?
Answer:  No eye deer (no idea).
1b. What do you call a deer with no eyes and no legs?
Answer: Still no eye deer.

2. Forwards, I'm heavy, but backwards I'm not. What am I?
Answer: A ton.

3. If you have it, you want to share it. If you share it, you don't have it.  What is it?
Answer: A secret.

4. In America, you cannot take a picture of a man with a sign. Why not?
Answer: You need a camera, not a sign, to take a picture.

5. The more you have of it, the less you see. What is it?
Answer: Darkness.

6. What is the middle of nowhere?
Answer: H.

7. What do you throw out when you want to use it, but take in when you don't want to use it?
Answer: An anchor.

8. Which letter is not me?
Answer: U.

9. Which is the most egoistic letter?
Answer: I.

10. What letter has the most amount of water?
Answer: C.

11. Who is bigger, Mr Bigger or Mr Bigger's son?
Answer: Mr Bigger's son, as he is a little Bigger.

12. Tom's mother has three children. One is named April, one is named May. What is the third one named?
Answer: Tom.

13. Two women apply for a job. They are identical. They have the same mother, father, birthdays, height, weight and so on. The interviewer asks, 'Are you twins?' They say, 'No.' Why did they say they weren't twins?
Answer: They were triplets – one of them wasn't there.

14. Why is a mathematics book always sad?
Answer: Because it is full of problems.

15. The one who made it didn't want it. The one who bought it didn't need it. The one who used it never saw it. What is it?
Answer: A coffin.

16. What can burn the eyes, sting the mouth, and yet be eaten?
Answer: A chilli pepper.

17. What crawls on four, then walks on two, then on three?
Answer: A person.

18. If your uncle's sister is related to you but is not your aunt, what relation is she?
Answer: Your mother.

19. Do you know if the Catholic church allows a man to marry his widow's sister?
Answer: A dead man cannot marry.

20. Can someone marry his brother's wife's mother in law?
Answer: A man cannot marry his own mother.

21. What are two things people don't eat before breakfast?
Answer: Lunch and dinner.

## Proverbs

A collection of proverbs for Pairs or Call My Bluff Definitions.

A bad penny always turns up.
A bad workman always blames his tools.
A bargain is something you don't need at a price you can't resist.
A bird in the hand is worth two in the bush.
A blessing in disguise.
A friend in need is a friend indeed.
A friend to all is a friend to none.
A jack of all trades is a master of none.
A little knowledge is a dangerous thing.
A miss is as good as a mile.
A penny saved is a penny earned.
A picture is worth a thousand words.
A rolling stone gathers no moss.
A stitch in time saves nine.
A watched pot never boils.
A woman's work is never done.
A word to the wise is sufficient.
Absence makes the heart grow fonder.
Actions speak louder than words.
All's fair in love and war.
All's well that ends well.
All roads lead to Rome.
All that glitters is not gold.
All things come to him who waits.
All work and no play.
An apple a day keeps the doctor away.

An eye for an eye and a tooth for a tooth.
April showers bring May flowers.
As fit as a fiddle.
Beauty is in the eye of the beholder.
Beauty is only skin deep.
Beggars can't be choosers.
Better late than never.
Better safe than sorry.
Better the devil you know than the one you don't.
Boys will be boys.
Birds of a feather flock together.
Blood is thicker than water.
Can't see the woods for the trees.
Charity begins at home.
Cleanliness is next to godliness.
Damned if you do and damned if you don't.
Don't bite the hand that feeds you.
Don't burn your bridges.
Don't count your chickens until they're hatched.
Don't cut off your nose to spite your face.
Don't judge a book by its cover.
Don't look a gift horse in the mouth.
Don't put all your eggs in one basket.
Don't throw the baby out with the bathwater.
There's no use crying over spilt milk.
Early to bed and early to rise.
Every cloud has a silver lining.
Familiarity breeds contempt.
First come first served.
First things first.
Fools rush in where angels fear to tread.
Good fences make good neighbours.
Go with the flow.
Give and take.
Great minds think alike.
Half a loaf is better than none.
Handsome is as handsome does.
He who generalizes generally lies.
Heaven helps those who help themselves.
Hell hath no fury like a woman scorned.

His bark is worse than his bite.
Honesty is the best policy.
Horses for courses.
Ignorance is bliss.
If a job is worth doing it's worth doing well.
If at first you don't succeed, try, try again.
If it ain't broke, don't fix it.
If you can't beat them, join them.
If you can't take the heat get out of the kitchen.
In for a penny, in for a pound.
It never rains, it pours.
It's better to have loved and lost than never to have loved at all.
It takes a thief to catch a thief.
It takes all sorts to make a world go round.
Learn to walk before you try to run.
Let sleeping dogs lie.
Life begins at 40.
Life is what you make of it.
Like father like son.
Like water off a duck's back.
Live and let live.
Look before you leap.
Love is blind.
Make hay while the sun shines.
Many hands make light work.
Mind your Ps and Qs.
Money for old rope.
Money can't buy happiness.
More haste less speed.
Necessity is the mother of invention.
No man is an island.
No pain, no gain.
Nothing ventured, nothing gained.
Once bitten, twice shy.
One man's meat is another man's poison.
Out of the frying pan, into the fire.
Out of sight, out of mind.
Patience is a virtue.
Power corrupts, absolute power corrupts absolutely.
Practice makes perfect.

Rome wasn't built in a day.
Seek and ye shall find.
Six of one and half a dozen of the other.
Sticks and stones may break my bones but words will never hurt me.
Speak of the devil.
Still waters run deep.
Strike while the iron is hot.
The ball is in your court.
The best is yet to come.
The best things in life are free.
The calm before the storm.
The early bird catches the worm.
The grass is always greener on the other side of the fence.
The pen is mightier than the sword.
The proof is in the pudding.
There are no endings, only new beginnings.
There are three types of lies – lies, damned lies and statistics.
There's a method to this madness.
There's more than one way to skin a cat.
There's no accounting for taste.
There's no rest for the wicked.
There's no place like home.
There's no such thing as a free lunch.
There's no room to swing a cat.
Think before you speak.
Time flies.
Time waits for no man.
To bark up the wrong tree.
To be born with a silver spoon in your mouth.
To each his own.
To dig yourself into a hole.
To keep up with the Joneses.
To kill the goose that lays the golden egg.
To know on which side your bread is buttered.
To make a mountain out of a molehill.
Tomorrow is another day.
To put your foot in it.
To talk the hind legs off a donkey.
Too many cooks spoil the broth.
Too many irons in the fire.

Two heads are better than one.
Two wrongs don't make a right.
Up a creek without a paddle.
Variety is the spice of life.
You can't have it both ways.
You can't have your cake and eat it.
You can't teach an old dog new tricks.
You can't win them all.
You made your bed so you must lie in it.
You reap what you sow.
You scratch my back and I'll scratch yours.
You win some, you lose some.
Waste not, want not.
We'll cross that bridge when we come to it.
What goes around comes around.
What goes up must come down.
What you see is what you get.
When in Rome, do as the Romans do.
When one door closes another one opens.
A wolf in sheep's clothing.

# 11
# APPENDIX

Please access the printable games that complement this book by filling in your email on the link below, or by emailing Shelley Ann Vernon on: info@teachingenglishgames.com.

**http://www.teachingenglishgames.com/receive-templates**

You will find blank templates as well as pre-filled examples for immediate use in class. Printable extras are provided for:

| | |
|---|---|
| A Day In The Life | Alibi |
| Alphabet War | Battleships |
| Build A Sentence | Connect Four |
| Cryptic Clues | Describe The Picture |
| English Trivia | Figure It Out |
| Find The Pairs | Gap Fill Game |
| How It's Made | Jeopardy |
| Parts Of Speech Pathfinder | Sequences |
| Spelling Challenge | Subject–Verb–Object |

Please also email me, Shelley Ann Vernon, at info@teachingenglishgames.com for help using any of the activities in this book or if you are stuck for ideas. I'm here to help and am looking forward to hearing from you.

## OTHER RESOURCES

I hope that this book of games brings much joy to your classrooms. If the comments I have had from hundreds of teachers are anything to go by, then it surely will. Here is some information about my other resources, which may be useful if you teach a variety of ages or class sizes.

### 1. 176 English Language Games For Children

This publication is on several Amazon websites (currently Amazon.com, Amazon.co.uk, Amazon.es, Amazon.fr, Amazon.de, Amazon.it, Amazon.ca, Amazon.jp, Amazon.in and Amazon.cn) as a physical book and as a Kindle. Search for 'ESL Games: English Language Games for Children Shelley Ann Vernon'.

### 2. Preschool Games And Stories 1 To 10

Ten stories covering basic vocabulary themes and useful vocabulary with a fun games book for pre-schoolers.

http://www.teachingenglishgames.com/esl-short-stories

### 3. English For Toddlers: How To Teach Nursery Kids English As A Second Language

### 4. Teaching English Songs 1, 2 And 3

This CD or download contains 16 songs to match the vocabulary taught in my preschool stories series. The words are simple and cover basic vocabulary themes, helping you to reinforce what you are teaching while bringing cheerful music to the classroom.

A songs activity book is included with CD 1, which includes lesson plan ideas for introducing and teaching each song. These may be used with any songs in the series. In addition, black-and-white masks for all the characters in the story are included, which can be cut out, coloured in and worn. Pre-coloured are also included.

www.teachingenglishgames.com/eslsongs.htm
www.teachingenglishgames.com/ESL-songs3

### 5.   10 x Follow-On Stories 11 To 20 With Lesson Plans

More stories covering actions, family members, rooms of the house, nature, light and dark, verbs, farm animals, body parts, clothing and other useful vocabulary.

www.teachingenglishgames.com/3-5/preschoolstories.htm

### 6.   10 x Stories For Special Days In The Year

Stories with lesson plans, flashcards, colouring and illustrations.

| | | |
|---|---|---|
| Birthday | Groundhog Day | April Fools' Day |
| Halloween | Valentine's Day | Mother's Day |
| Thanksgiving | Easter Bunny | Summer Holiday |
| Adventure | | |
| Christmas | | |

Includes revision of vocabulary and grammar from stories 1 to 20, plus new words, language and tenses.

www.teachingenglishgames.com/eslstory.htm

### 7.   Stories For Young Primary School Children

Stories with lesson plans, flashcards and worksheets covering talking about yourself, descriptions, places, school, sports, weather, body parts, the house and furniture, daily routine, and fruit and vegetables.

http://www.teachingenglishgames.com/esl-stories-for-children

## 8. One-To-One Games And Video

Games for private tutors and parents with video demonstrations for ages 4 to 12.

www.homeenglishteacher.com

## 9. Plays And Skits For Children

Plays and skits for small groups of up to 15 students, or bigger classes if you have good classroom management and can manage groups of children working separately. For beginners aged 4 to 12. Private tutors or parents may also use these for one-on-one teaching. These simple, repetitive skits with a touch of humour are easily adapted to higher levels.

www.teachingenglishgames.com/eslplays.htm

## ABOUT THE AUTHOR

Following her BA degree in languages at Durham University, England, in 1989 Shelley Vernon took a TEFL qualification and became a teacher. She taught in language schools in the UK and privately around the world for several years.

Having been largely bored to death herself while in school, Shelley was determined not to put her own students through the same desperate clock watching, and she always strove to prepare fun, stimulating lessons that pupils would enjoy and remember. She taught using a variety of methods, including the driest textbooks imaginable, which called for large amounts of creativity in order to make lessons more interesting. However, it was only when she started to teach children French as a second language in 1999 that she really discovered the joy of teaching.

She created a method from her experiences and has shared her ideas with thousands of teachers around the world, bringing enthusiasm and a love of learning into the classroom, as well as achieving great results. Shelley's approach concentrates on enhancing listening and speaking skills through language games that involve repetition and through fluency activities that have genuine communicative value rather than enforcing artificial conversation.

She created her bestselling *English Language Games for Children* and followed this with resources for pre-school children, including games and a curriculum laid out in 20 illustrated stories. Having taught pre-school children at a Montessori nursery school, Shelley knows exactly what a teacher needs to be successful, and stories are a stunningly useful element. Her *ESL Games and Activities for Adults* are also highly praised by teachers around the world.

In addition to her degree in foreign languages, Shelley holds a university degree in music (2000) from Canterbury Christchurch College. She loves classical music, and enjoys keeping fit with skiing, yoga and walking her adorable cocker spaniel. She also writes songs and has produced three pre-school songs CDs. She occasionally speaks at conferences such as IATEFL Cardiff 2009, YALS Belgrade 2011, UCN, Hjorring, Denmark 2014 and Barcelona in 2015.

Shelley Ann Vernon

## ACKNOWLEDGMENTS

Since the first edition of this book many teachers have written to me with stories of their successes, adaptations and game ideas. With each new edition improvements have been made based on those practical tips and recommendations. Many thanks therefore to all the teachers who wrote to me with ideas, stories and classroom fun, which can now be shared with you.

INDEX OF GAMES IN ALPHABETICAL ORDER